God's Protective Sign

Finding Faith & Forgiveness and Drive on.

Table of Contents

Dedication

First giving God all the glory and the praise for allowing me to share my gift with others is truly an absolute honor. Eight months was perfect because it allowed me time to finalize this project. I dedicate my book to my husband, Darryl D. Williams who have been by my side from the thought of writing to the production of the finished product.

To our five children Derrick, Darion, Denyata, DJ, & Donte I pray that someday you too will share this with your children: my two granddaughters London J. Dwight & Peyton E. Guinyard, my grandsons Eli J. Guinyard and Logan A. Dwight always remember that a star is born inside of all of us. God created each one of you to bring greatness into the world so,

I challenge you to never give up when you're feeling down, stop, rest and start all over again.

To my parents, Mr. Ralph & Thelmer Dwight of Elloree, South Carolina every time I think about how good God has been to our family as he empowered me to do more. You are my idols and without your endless guidance, I don't know where I would be today. To my mother and father in law, Mr. Nathaniel & Geneva Deveaux of Burton, South Carolina, Christ lives in both of you so that only goodness will continue to overflow your hearts and affect everyone you meet. Thank you for all the support and prayers sealed with your everlasting love.

Love is the greatest gift of all, so I pray that this book helps you to find your way, strengthen your faith and allow you to continue to give love even

when other may hate!

This book is dedicated to young single mothers of all ages, who have felt they had no one they could trust, while experiencing difficult times in their lives even if that point happens to be right now. A female born of a man's rib has a curvature appearance to it and may appear to be easily broken; despite its image, it is as strong as it looks. Often the breakage comes at midpoint because the ends are made much more rigid and harder to grasp.

One must manipulate it repeatedly before it starts to lose its density and become frail and weak. The old saying is that when a bone breaks, it never heals the same. Even when a mirror shatters it breaks into smaller pieces but the glory of it all is that you can still see your self-worth therefore; let no one think that he or she can easily break you.

That's why God's Protective Signs allows you to look beyond the shattered glass, pick up the solid pieces and a few with jaggered edges just as a reminder that time heals all wounds. Reset your GPS and continue going through personal life experiences including these signs into your everyday life. If you've suffered physically, mentally and or emotionally stop everything and say to yourself, "Who Am I Not to Be, If Only You Could See What I See in Me... I may be broken but, I'm still a beautiful child of GOD blessed with faith, favour and forgiveness and yes, I Am Somebody"!!!!!!

Introduction

The moment you were created became the discovery of a new beginning. Throughout your time spent in the womb, it's possible that you have been centered, cornered, and or pushed in a direction that often was uncomfortable, challenging, unsecured or even rewarding. Upon your arrival, a team of doctors, nurses, specialists, social worker's, other professionals, and most importantly your parent(s) defined an outline providing the essentials that's normally required to aid in your developmental stages. These steps I call are directions.

On June 20, 1970 at Nassau County Medical Center in New York at 1:14pm, God brought me into this world with a fulfilled purpose. Hours after a series of test, x-rays & scans my mother was informed that I had a bowel obstruction. My new beginning started off rough, so one would think that my life would only get easier. Today, I'm looking back over my past that held many imperfections, the present to explore my possibilities, and into my future to enhance my God given talents to utilize my personal inspirations and life coaching skills to help guide youths, single parents, and families to live a productive lifestyle that gives them a better sense of self. Also, to help them develop a creative niche, and the ability to make ethical and moral decisions that would foster growth in their personal lives and prospective career choices.

God's Protective Signs is a glimpse of my life through my own eyes and experiences that I've encountered as a child, teenager, friend, single parent, college student, business owner, wife, police officer, stepmom, inspirational speaker and a life coach. I've traveled along many roadways, highways, over and under bridges and around the mountains in all climates of weather. I've approached obstacles and have faced numerous challenges; but God took the wheel and has always been the driver of my vehicle(s), the motorcycle, the moped, the bicycle, the go cart, the buses, and the airplanes. I'm truly blessed by his Grace and mercy to have withstand all my challenges thus far!

Now, I understand why the devil is always putting up road blocks & barriers. It's simply because he has manipulated the minds of many people in believing that he cares more about them than anybody else and uses their personal rejections as a reason why they should not have any ethical or moral boundaries. The devil will not bother those who choose to stand for something positive in life.

You see, sometimes when a person falls short and loses his or her focus on what's pertinent in their lives, such as their children, families, and or true friends; the lack of money to sustain stability or living in an undesirable neighborhood that's infested with illegal activities which often leads them to being easily influenced that causes them more harm than good. Truth be told, the moment he or she allows their tongue to confess their sins and ask God for forgiveness, they too will be given a new lease on life with all expenses paid in full and a new direction of travel.

No one is perfect, but everyone should want to try to be the best they can be. So, when you've fallen and need help getting back up-take one arm and pull yourself up to a kneeling position and then ask God to help you stand on your feet again. Remember, the only way one can fail something is that he or she never tries anything.

Family is everything, love one another as God so loves us!

Caution

Have you thanked the Almighty Father this morning? Last night? Any time this week? Okay, we have some work to do. Yes, I said "we", there have been times when I would be caught up in the moment or might I add, when things are going well, I forget to acknowledge him. I'm guilty of that myself. The way things are in this world we live in I must say to each one of you to take caution. Understand that God deserves all the Glory every day. Joy is a feeling, I believe we all long to have more of. So why isn't this happening? I'll tell you what I think, the devil been planning his escapades and lurking in the dark to prey on the weakest souls.

Case and point: a well-rounded two parent family with employment making just above minimum wages, when suddenly one has been laid off due to budget cuts around the time a new addition is expected to be added to the family. All the bills start mounting up and the stress becomes the center of attention in the relationship. Now the adults are at odds and not speaking to one another. The children are not clearly understanding

Caution

why they cannot continue with extra curriculum activities at school. After a couple of weeks that built-up pressure turns into a medical problem. Hypertension is one of the top issues easily seen. And now family members are siding with the spouse that still has income, coaching them to put their spouse out. Talking about added pressure. That partner does not deal with rejection well, so he or she decides to walk away from the family, feeling like a failure and imagine that the family would be better off without them.

Nowhere to turn and no place to hide. Suddenly they're singled out and approached by a stranger with caution that has a similar story to share. The two walks off into the darkness and left the world behind them. Several hours later, they don't even remember how they ended up in a dark place alone with a stranger; but what is remembered they had alienated those daunting feelings of failure and now their new job is a must have and that's getting the next "fix" to keep on forgetting anything else exists!

Caution

One should stop and think that there's nothing in this world that is more self-sacrificed than the blood of Jesus Christ. He can and will help you through your darkness hours; he can cleanse your soul, but you must confess and ask God for forgiveness. Power is in the tongue! He can clean you whiter than snow. Trust in him and believe that he is the Father (the truth), the Son (the way), and the Holy Spirit (the light). Glory be to the Father. It doesn't matter about your past situation or your current situation if you have faith in him, he can fix it!

A blind man cannot see, but his ears could tell the entire story. I was a six-year-old spirited little girl just full of energy and always out to explore the simpler things life had to offer back in the mid 70's. I always believed that I could grow as tall as the elevators. In my apartment complex in Hempstead, we only had six levels. On this day, the clouds looked tired as if was it was telling the sky to bring

Caution

on the rain. My best friend was away so, I was bored and decided that I would get all the free rides I could get before it was time to go inside for the night.

I pressed the buttons so many times, I started acting like an operator on a busy hotline. Up and down I rode. One stop a lady got on and asked if I was lost. I told her that my mommy knew where I was, so she departed without further questioning. Next few minutes no stops and I felt like I was sitting on top of the world all by myself. When the elevator was heading back down to the third floor, it stopped, and the doors opened, and a young teenager appeared. He greeted me with a smile. As the doors began to close he grabbed me around my upper body and

Caution

tried to lower me to the floor. I began kicking and screaming than he placed his hand over my mouth, although it smelled like an ashtray, I bit down on his finger as hard as I could. I was too scared to cry; I knew I had to get away from him. I was reaching for the door and he kept trying to pull me back. The doors were attempting to close, but each time I got closer and closer.

All I could think about was if my mother found out that I was really playing on the elevator, how severe my punishment would be. So, I continued fighting and then it happened. An old man heard all the commotion just outside his apartment and when he peaked outside his door he sensed that someone was in serious trouble. The young man was desperately

Caution

trying to remove my pants. This old man

approached the elevator's door and with both of his

hands raised he began hitting the young man with

his walking cane. Yelling in an authoritative voice,

let her go before I kill you! Moments later, I was

freed feeling confused and afraid. The only thing I

wanted to do was to be taller than the elevator not

lowered beneath self-worth and taken advantage of.

What that young man didn't know was that this nice

old man was blind. All the tenants that heard about

this incident could not identify this teenager as a

tenant living there. That nice old man was my hero.

He stopped what could have been the start of a life

that I never dreamed of nor was prepared to deal

with. He made sure that I got back to my apartment

safe. I hope that you all don't think that the rest of

Caution

my evening/night ended that easily. He was compelled to tell my mother about this near horrific experience. Let's just say that after my mother made a police report and made certain that I was fine, fed, bathe and given a few more hours to settle down; she offered me a special treat that wasn't candy or cookies, but flavor for my soul!

If you're thinking oh my, well back than I felt the same way, but today as I speak about that isolated incident from the struggle for dear life in the elevator and the consequences of not obeying my mother as a child supposed too. This was the beginning of me accepting that I must stand up for everything that's right and never fall for anything that is wrong. Mother, I say Thank You. And her way of assuring me that this incident would ever happen again, she packed my clothes and contacted two of my uncles and they drove from South Carolina to Hempstead, New York to get me out of there. I then became a two-pigtail wearing little southern girl. My mother stayed behind to tie up loose ends and her plans were to get out of the city as soon as she could. The summer was near over, and my grandmother had a massive heart attack, so my mother dropped everything and moved to South Carolina to help care for her.

Growing up in a rural town as a child, I looked forward to the weekends because my mother and her sisters would have family gatherings at my aunt's house sitting around my great grandmother

Caution

bedside and reminiscing about their childhood days. One day while sitting in grown up company, I noticed a ladybug crawling on great grandma. I asked my mom to get it off her and she looked at me and said, "Denise I don't see no bug, get up and gone outside and play with the other kids". I got up and said, but ma...it's right there as I pointed to it. So, my aunt thought that I was playing around and just seeing things. I was serious y'all, it was a red ladybug with black dots on its' back. Grandma Noxie said leave that child alone so moments later they got up and walked out still chatting about their own conversation. Grandma Noxie said, "baby close the door". I stood at her bedside and continue to watch the ladybug as it crawled over her night gown near her chest area. She said get it, I leaned in

Caution

and allow it to crawl onto the back of my hand and I present it as if it had won first place.

She told me to sit, as I walked to sit back in the chair, she said no and patted on the bed as my clue to sit next to her. I took that seat feeling a bit nervous after all, I was only thirteen. She spoke in a soft tone, but her message was loud and clear. Grandma Noxie told me that I was the chosen one. I pointed towards myself and nodded, and she said, yes baby. She continues to explain that this ladybug had black spots and each one will represent some of the darkest times in my life and the redness represents the color of my heart in which I will always find strength & courage to overcome it. She added, that I will grow to become the women that

Caution

God has created me to be. So, I asked why me grandma? She replied, baby many are born, but a few are chosen and to be blessed with this special gift, why not you? Yes ma'am, I replied. So, grandma is this ladybug real, yes baby it is. Why couldn't they see it? Because things unseen is not always believable. I was still confused because I believed what I saw, I held it, and I let it go. Now thinking back over all that I had gone through to get where I am today, finally I got it! All my trials and tribulations, I didn't foresee them coming, but I dealt with them from begin to end and I was able to forgive and move forward in faith. This was God's plan for my life. I'm strong just like the rib that I was made of. I've grown into a beautiful black woman who lives a positive lifestyle. I'll continue to strive for higher altitude because my life has been at its' lowest level. Now when I see ladybugs, I feel empowered. I have three ladybugs tattooed on my right foot one red and the other two are blue ones, they represent my three born children. I say thank you great grandma Noxie, for sharing kind words of wisdom with me. She passed away in 1987.

I had the privilege of working in the family business. Pic N Go Saving Furniture Store located on Cleveland Street in Elloree, South Carolina; the only black family own business in town. It was very competitive but with the hard work and perseverance the business was a success. We had new customers patronizing the store on a weekly basis because we offered the best prices in town.

Caution

Some of the other local businesses would have random people walk into our establishment pretending to show interest in some of the merchandise, but little that they knew God had if fixed that through conversation, they would reveal the real purpose for their visit. They were bribed to pose as a secret shopper and in return they were

given a free chicken basket with a soft drink. Curiosity could have killed the cat, but instead we fed them too. I used to work three days a week after school. I realized after several months of working part time; I enjoyed interacting with other people, but selling furniture wasn't exactly my creative niche.

Caution

My step-dad became my best male friend simply because he took time to listen to me and talk to me. He was also an extraordinary cook. I must say that my biological father, the late Mr. Willie Lee Gidron, played a major role in my life until his unexpected demised. He died when I was only six years of age. I often think about the times we spent together at the ball games. When people saw us together they would say, that's Willie's daughter right there she looks just like him. He died of a heart attack while getting into his car one Sunday morning. I remember vividly that day, my mother was giving me a bath when my cousin ran over to grandma house and said, Aunt Thelmer, Denise father died today. My mom tried not to let her emotions show; but I could tell that it made her sad.

Caution

I remember asking her if my daddy was going to still pick me up and she said that God needed him to do something special for him that day. I wasn't sure if I understood what that meant, so I figured that he would come once he got finished. Later, that night my mother was talking with her sister and she said that my daddy was resting. I was mad because he forgot to come and get me, so I started crying and my aunt heard me. She called out to me and said, baby don't cry your daddy loved you so much and he will always be with you in your heart. No auntie, I know he loves me, but why did he go to sleep. I want to call and wake him up. She looked down at the floor and paused briefly. My mother walked out of the room. Auntie said, sweetie your daddy is an angel now. He is with the Lord; but you can still

Caution

talk to him anytime you want to, and he will help
God watch over you and keep you safe. I closed my
eyes and looked up to the ceiling and whispered
daddy please call me because I miss you.

My parents provided all our basic needs as we were
growing up. They instilled love, faith, morals &
values, respect and patience within us. My siblings
and I never created big trouble as teenagers leading
us into young adulthood. Our upbringing holds true
to this day!

We are a family filled with unconditional love. My
mother is a beautiful black queen in my eyes. She
knows how to care for her husband, children, home,
the business and yet still finds time to spend quality
time with us. Her health began to weaken in the late

Caution

nineties. She had a stroke which limited her abilities for nearly six months. She endured weeks of rehabilitation in the hospital and continued physical therapy upon her return home for another six months.

My step-dad took time off from his workplace as a foreman for one of North Carolina's largest construction companies caring for my mother and maintaining the family business as well. This was emotionally and physically stressful which started to take a toll on him, but he never complained. Although, I wasn't old enough, I felt as though I had to step up an assist with managing our home, my school work, caring for my mother, and the family business. My siblings felt the same way.

Caution

Together we worked as a team around the home inside and out. Our parents made certain that they did everything humanly possible to support us, so that we would never have to worry about our necessities being met and often we receive many extras for good behavior. Shortly after my mother's health progressed, she slowly glided back into the workplace. I guess from all the stress that he collected finally showed up and presented itself as he began experiencing heart problems. A hard-working devoted husband and father who smoked cigarettes to calm his nerves during the work week and boost his energy to keep the store stocked with top of the line furniture on the weekends. Smoking has not been the single factor for his underlying heart problems, but most definitely an important

Caution

one to consider. Stress and Hypertension played a vital role as well. Years of juggling the job, the family, the home, and the business lead to more frequent doctor's appointments, emergency room visits, constant changing of medications, a change in dietary, and disruptive of sleep patterns placed a tremendous strain on him which caused a downward spiral of our family's financial stability. He kept the faith and kept on working. It seems as things couldn't get any worse, my mother had a second stroke. The stress began to have a domino effect on me because I felt like I was going in circles. By this time, I'm a teenager and my siblings have graduated from high school, so they started working fulltime at the company my step dad worked for. All hope wasn't lost so, I became the

Caution

eyes and hears of the house. My job was to keep the

family members informed of my parent's progress.

You see, I was the one that the doctors would

explain everything to and then I would convey that

information in its' simplest form whereas; my

parents would understand it. You may be asking

yourself how she could know this if she's just a

teenager. Well, let's just say that God blesses the

child who has its' own. My computer became my

personal dictionary. I believed that I've learned

more online than I did in my eighth-grade health

class. No offense, I really liked my Health Science

teacher, Ms. Hewitt. As time moved forward, both

of my parents' health continued to seesaw over the

next several years. If my mother was admitted into

the hospital for stroke like activity in her brain, it

Caution

seemed like my step dad's heart condition would manage to stay stabilized until she could get home. Once he knew she was feeling a little better, within a few days, he would be admitted in the hospital for observation, testing, or same day surgeries.

I recalled him asking the doctor during one of his hospital stays, if his old ticker didn't get better and a heart transplant would be required, did he think that he would lose his passion for cooking? The doctor looked at him and replied, well now, I can't really answer that one. Over a period, the nursing staff in the emergency department could almost calculate my parent's visits and was able to recognize them on a first name basis. My step-dad with his heart condition and my mother kept having

Caution

multiple mini strokes also known as TIA's causing her brain to become affected on both sides was scary. I can still recall hearing her doctor say that if she has one more "stroke" it could be the one to immobilize her or be the cause of her death. That day wasn't like any other day after hearing those words. The doctor stated for us to take *caution* and monitor her daily activities, dieting and any signs/symptoms that may appeared to alter her mental state. That evening my step-dad held a family meeting to discuss my mother's current health condition and ways we could help prevent anymore stroke attacks even though he too had serious health problems. The next day was a new beginning; he started things off with nutritional meals three times a day. I added more of running the business to my schedule (5 days) a week after school. My siblings took over the house chores and manage the bills. Yes, they made big bucks back then and things weren't as expensive as they are now.

My step-dad and I made home visits to customers who had missed their scheduled monthly payments to try and bring their accounts current. Some customer's thought that due to my mother's illness they could write off the balance that was rightfully owed. Sorry to be the bearer of bad news, she's alive and well and the written agreement was still in full effect. We repossessed a lot of merchandise for non-payment.

Caution

My step-dad and I would go to the auctions on some Saturday mornings looking for more unique styles. This was a field trip for me. I clearly enjoyed myself. I loved listening to the auctioneer conduct the bidding process. It tickled me trying to figure out what he was saying. We made several big purchases over the next couple of years and the business was back on track, however; enough fun and games reality kicked back in when my mother's health took another turn downhill. Yes, she had another stroke. Oh, how frantic we became knowing what the doctor already told us. Everyday thereafter, we grew more restless until suddenly it happened…. our Heavenly Father became well known to my family again in body, mind & spirit. He showed us how wonderful and how great he

Caution

truly is. Prayer changes things and he changed her direction from sickness to healing. Three more months of rehab and she's still alive and well. My mother had three strokes that were confirmed based on the Computerized Tomography (CT) scans and Magnetic Resonance Imaging (MRI) test. Her brain on one side has been greatly affected. The physicians were at awe because they haven't seen it quite like that before and each time she managed to bounce back stronger and stronger. My step-dad decided to retire my mother and close the family business because nothing materialistic is worth having more of than your love ones. She has a testimony and I'm honored to be able to share her personal challenges. Her faith keeps me believing in things unseen. My mother had her fourth stroke.

Caution

She spent only four days in the hospital and six days at the nursing home for rehabilitation. God is still an awesome God! Remember, I said that my step-dad had a heart condition-well his health also took a drastic turn downhill. He needed a heart transplant after years long of being in and out of the hospitals, and doctors' offices. Now, it appears any and everything was affecting his heart. I know that God had just brought my mother through another rough trial. I was praying that he was still on the main line, so that I could tell him what I wanted again. In 2008, several hearts crossed-matched, but had some aliments that were not acceptable by the team of surgeons and or by my step-dad. One heart was a perfect match, but the donor tested positive for HIV. My step dad refused that heart because he felt that

Caution

just knowing that information it would worry him to

death. Things were looking bad and my step-dad

was so sick, he was medevac to The Medical

University of Charleston in Charleston, South

Carolina.

The head surgeon informs our family that time was

racing against us and he needed a heart very soon or

the possibility of my step-dad's discharge from the

hospital would be rolled out on a gurney. There was

not another heart in the hospital that was a cross-

match. He also stated that my step-dad was placed

on the A-1 donor's list. I looked deep into my

mother's eyes, I saw a vulnerable woman who had

beaten all odds begin to slowly allow hope and faith

to disappear from her mind; but I interceded before

Caution

it could slip from her heart. Mommy, I called out to

her…listen to me. My voice began to crackle, but I

knew I had to stay calm and strong for them.

Mommy, I shrugged her shoulders, God is the head

surgeon and the one thing that we know for sure is

that the heart he still has holds the power of "love".

He is going to make it! The surgeon looked at me

with a stern face and said, "please tell God that

myself and this entire staff here at MUSC is sending

up our prayers as well". I knew that God didn't

bring us this far to leave us now. I specifically

asked God to prepare a heart and a room to perform

this surgery of a miracle on my step-dad. On

October 9, 2008, around 8:30pm the drive from the

hospital was as silent as a single prayer at the altar.

We arrived back home, and I'd just walked into the

Caution

house heading towards the kitchen when the telephone rang. It felt like my heart stopped, because my brain was losing oxygen quickly, it felt like everything around me became a blur. The second ring jump started my heart to beating faster and I was able to breathe again. It was beating so fast, I felt my heart inside of my throat. It was so close to my head, I could hear it loud and clear in my eardrum. I grabbed the receiver and struggled to say hello and then it happened.... I heard the doctor's voice and it was filled with joy. He said hello, is this Mrs. Dwight? I replied, no sir, its Mr. Dwight's daughter. He replied, I have great news, a heart was flown in minutes after you departed from the hospital and the reason it took so long to call you was because I needed to make certain that it's a

Caution

cross-match. I couldn't believe what I was hearing. My mother was standing there leaning against the wall trying to embrace for the worse. That's when I yelled out "momma, they found a heart, they found a heart"! My step-dad's surgery was scheduled for 10:15 pm that same night. I knew God heard my desperate cry and that he was going to make everything alright.

The morning of October 10, 2008 at approximately 6:11am ironically is the same time my oldest son was born on my step-dad's birthday; he was rolled out of the operating room surrounded by a team of surgeons dressed in long white coats looking like angels God sent from heaven. We were giving a

Caution

split second to see him before being taken to the recovery room. God is simply amazing!

Two hard working adults only tried providing for their children played the cards they were dealt. Among those cards was the king and queen of hearts, and it was played right on time. When the head surgeon walked into the family room where we were placed, he delivered the news we longed to hear, but he also added that he wanted me to do the honors of informing my step-dad that the new heart he received came from a thirty-five-year-old male whose occupation was a chef in California. Tears ran down my face, no more holding them back. My family and I was going to be alright. God made

Caution

another way out of no way. There wasn't a day that
went by, have I ever heard either one of them
complain. Through all the support, acts of kindness
and prayers, love preceded them all. Our bodies are
only as strong as the mind thinks it should be. I say
to each one of you reading my story when you see
the caution light flashing-slow down and take a
second or third look before proceeding on through.
Your health is paramount. Their trials are now
triumphs and let their voices continue to shout glory
halleluiah that victory is theirs!

You cannot change the past, but you can control

your future!

No "U" Turn

Leaving middle school was bitter-sweet. In 1984, I
was honored to have had the opportunity to be
crowned Miss Saint John Middle School. My aunt
Anna made the dresses for me and my court for the
homecoming parade. Looking back at this
prestigious title only made me realize that my
attitude reflected my leadership. High school was
another stepping stone to reach and unlocking the
doors to my future. Academically, I never had any
problems with making good grades, making friends,
following instructions and or participating in extra
curriculum activities. I was always willing to
challenge myself to see just how far I could go. I
played junior varsity basketball. I was a member on
the band, the clarinet was my instrument of choice.
I joined the JROTC. I made the varsity cheerleading

No "U" Turn

squad. I was the teacher's pet in my English class and always willing to help my fellow classmates in any way that I could. I had great final four years of high school, but there was one occurrence that continues to keep me grounded until this day. I was willing to take a stand for a friend who was shy and appeared vulnerable. I decided to address an ongoing concern that left a friend feeling as if she didn't belong. She was often bullied by other students. I was not going to stand by and do nothing. Enough is enough I said. Bullying is a learned behavior, so I took a candid approach and confronted two sisters one morning, while they sat in the cafeteria eating breakfast together. A verbal dispute quickly erupted and as the crowd began to gather around us, I grabbed a fork off one of the

No "U" Turn

food trays because I noticed that they were preparing to stand up and the word was, they often fought together. However, it never got physical. I was scooped up and carried from the cafeteria by the head football coach while other students attempted to detain the two sisters. I saw them again out in the hallway and my words became a missile aiming directly them. I made this statement: "It doesn't matter where I see you I going to get you, I promise". Well, timely enough the principal was walking up the hallway and he heard my direct threat. Seconds later, I was in the office. My parents were called, and I was given in school suspension for the remainder of that day; but I could not return to school without a board review because of my verbal threat. I was facing possible explosion. Now,

No "U" Turn

that I'm calming down, I realized that its two weeks away from my high school graduation and my future may be placed on hold because of a decision I made based on "hearsay". Everything that happened that morning went against what was instill in me as a child growing up. My parents wanted to gather all the facts before rendering any form of punishment. Wow, this was something I really should have thought about first. So, that afternoon while sitting in the reality room for the remaining if the day, my mind was thinking about the consequences once I got home. I knew I was going to be reminder of who I am, what I stood for, and what I was sent to school for every day. The other students including my friend joined me in the reality room for in school detention. The reality

No "U" Turn

room was designed for students to reflect on their conduct and attitudes and to focus on their studies plus complete additional assignments that was added by their teachers which had to be turned in by the end of the week. The teacher often left the classroom and we took it upon ourselves to find out, who said what. Through several small hand notes being passed around in secrecy, it was clear that the information I received was all wrong. The one who told me the information made up the statement because she knew I would defend my friend. In all actuality, she had a problem with the sisters and was afraid to approach them on her own terms. I swallowed my pride and apologized and ask for their forgiveness, they accepted it. My friend apologized as well and thanked me for defending

No "U" Turn

her. I had determined that "hearsay" was the beginning and the end of me ever partaking in any third-party discussions ever again. Lesson well learned that if you don't hear the information with your own two ears, think twice about reacting or approaching the alleged source. Because in the end you are the one left with the problem. I never had any other discipline issues in school therefore; I was granted the opportunity to complete my senior year as long as I avoided trouble. The turning point of high school for me was learning from my mistakes on a smaller scale and accepting the weight that held me down even if though it was just for a little while. Always develop good character and lead by example. As for the parties involved in my escapade, we all became good friends. Your past

No "U" Turn

may or may not affect your future success, but
everyone has a way of finding out the simplest
details of your life. You can try to erase your past,
but the marks are still there waiting for you or
someone else to reprint them. In June 1988, I
graduated along with my senior class. Many years
after graduation one of the two sisters married a
relative of mines and during one of their home visits
here in South Carolina, she stopped by to see me.
We laughed about our past and thanked God for
how he brought us through.

Our lives were filled with so much love, peace and
happiness. I remember her saying thank you. I
asked, what did I do to deserve that? She stated that
back in high school, she did have a bad attitude and

No "U" Turn

the reputation that she and her sister were labeled
with really wasn't who she wanted to be. The
incident that occurred between us truly made her
realizes that she needed to change her personal
ways. Little that anyone could have imagined later
that night while they were driving back to their
home another vehicle drifted into their lane killing
them in a head-on collision. I was devastated!
Saying sorry wasn't good enough. God will see you
dealing with a situation and when it gets out of
hand, he will step right in and take control.

I'm so grateful I saw her that day, but I never
thought that it would be our last visit together. Life
is too short, today everyone may not have had this

No "U" Turn

day to make things right and tomorrow is not

promised to any of us.

Slowing down allows you to take a closer look at what

matters most in your life!

Yield

Have you ever been face with so many decisions to make, but undecided on which way to go? Thinking that if you go right it's wrong or if you go left than what are my chances. Have you ever considered to just slow down and allow things that you cannot control pass by you? Keep on moving until you find out that your FAITH will guide you away from unwanted traffic and onto route **7** that will run towards your destination. Make sure that you fasten your seatbelts and adjust your headrest because the ride will not be the smoothest. Along the way, you will see potholes ahead in the road that will remind you of people that wants to try and hold you down, simply because they aren't motivators, they are your haters'.

Route **7** is a highway that is mostly used by individuals willing to cast all their doubts about life expectancies onto it because this highway has a built-in **GPS** (God Protective Signs) which never fails nor leads you into the wrong direction. Again, you will often run into more obstacles such as a one lane closed sign ahead due to construction: or should I say, so called friends doing everything to keep you close enough to them to stop you in your tracks from being successful. There's no reason to get discouraged, all you must do is pull into the rest area and acknowledge the presence of the Lord. He will give you the strength and assurance you need to drive on. Trust and believe God sees and knows it all.

Can someone else define your fate? Is it okay to judge others? What would Jesus do? Faith is not purchasable; it comes from within. Faith is a combination of the mind, body, and soul working together to build a solid foundation with the Supreme Being. He provides all your needs, and he is always on time. So, to answer the first two question asked at the beginning of this paragraph- "No". Jesus died for all our sins on the cross, so you don't owe anybody anything except yourself to be all that you can be.

Let your beauty shine through the meanest things that could be said about you. Silence usually startles a person to stop and reevaluate their next move. So, no matter what trials or tribulations you are going through, God delivered David and he can deliver you. Meanwhile, you have joy, peace and love all around you and they are miserable. Remember, never stop only slow down to give God the right

Yield

away to be the head of your life! I challenged myself again during my junior year. I became a student school bus driver. Yes, as a teenager I anticipated the feeling of taking on another huge responsibility such as transporting children to and from school this was the biggest accomplishment by far. I was nervous and excited, but I refused to allow any task to defeat me.

I was placed with the adults for the training. My fellow classmates were group together. I wanted to ask why I wasn't training with them, but I didn't. The trainer must have had physic abilities because he came to me and said that he felt I was more mature and focused and that he only works with those he knows will take his training very seriously.

Well, his guess was right, I passed without any points against me. This was better than getting my driver's license. I drove my route up until I was forced to quit. Yes, I was a junior in high school, unwed and pregnant. I knew that my body was changing, and I missed several periods yet in my

Yield

mind, I did not want to accept the fact that I was pregnant. I was too afraid to tell my mother because everything that I was taught about abstinence and safe sex, I totally disregarded them. My parent's use to be at work a lot and that only gave me more free time on my hands after school.

Understand my household had standards, and we lived by them for the most part, but I was sixteen, what was a girl too do? My boyfriend was the love of my life and my best friend. He used to ride his bicycle almost ten miles one way just to see me on any given hot summer day. When my mom did find out she was devastated, many nights I sat in my closet and cried and cried hating myself, and then I started blaming my boyfriend because he promised

Yield

that nothing like this would happen. My mother

took me to the doctor and she was told that I was

five months. She said because I made my bed hard

now was the time that I had to lay in it. I made some

choices in life that I truly do regret, but my children

are not one of them. The doctor that delivered me

had doubts about me ever being able to bear

children; but my heavenly father saw otherwise.

Nowadays, children under age are caring for

siblings while mom is either at work, at a party,

with a man, hanging with her friends or spaced out

of her mind. Daddy's are bout his business too, his

cars, money, drugs, chasing women or simply

unknown. Not all parent's fall into this life style,

but the numbers are alarming for those that do.

Females give yourself time to grow and

Yield

mature before making selfish acts that will cause you to have to struggle and even worse, have an abortion or place your child up for adoption. I was fortunate enough to have parents and siblings that did not turn their backs on me. They gave me tough love, but what's so important is that over time it made me become the mother I am today.

My oldest son Derrick was born October 24th on my step-dad's birthday. I had the love and support from my family and limited friends. I had limited friends because back than some of the parents and other people felt that a single young black female having babies would never amount to

Yield

anything in life. Well, I didn't try to appease

others by saying that they were right about

my life, but a year later, I gave birth to

another baby boy named Darion. I had just

recently graduated from high school and still

living in my parents' house. Most people

had their assumptions about what could I

have been thinking and how would I manage

to care for two children and whether their

father was involved in their lives. Well yes,

he was a part of their lives and he worked in

construction to help support them. He loved

his sons and whatever he had they got. I

received six welfare checks totaling less

than one hundred and ten dollars per month.

I knew that it wasn't enough to live off

Yield

being a single parent. Understand when I
said single, I was not married to their father
and despite what he had to offer, I was
determined to be the best mother I could be.
I found employment at the local farmer's
market in Columbia, South Carolina where I
worked for five and a half years. Things
weren't the best, but better than they were
before. October 1991, I became pregnant
again with my third child and a new baby
daddy. This time I was having a baby girl
and I named her Denyata. Still as a single
parent; I had to work even harder to provide
for my babies. By this time, I was working
as a certified nursing assistant at a local
hospital. On October 5, 1997, my sons'

Yield

father was shot and killed by a South
Carolina State Trooper. Another setback in
our lives. What am I going to do now? His
life mattered. The image is still fresh in my
mind. It was close to the end of my shift
when my pager started going off none stop. I
did not answer because I didn't recognize
the numbers, plus I was too focus on getting
a slice of pizza from the staff in the
emergency department. As I stood there
waiting patiently for it, I heard the message
over the scanner loud and clear. It
announced the ambulance number, their
estimate time of arrival (ETA) and added,
please be advised that there's no need to
setup triage because they had a black male,

Yield

approximately 20-25 years of age dead on

arrival (DOA). I quietly said to myself, "Oh

Lord, another black man gone; my heart

goes out to his family". Minutes later, I had

divulged two slices of pizza and a cup of

Pepsi soda. Suddenly, I heard my name

called out across the intercom stating that I

needed to report to Two East (Pediatrics

Unit). I looked down at my watch and

noticed that I only had minutes' left before

my shift was ending so what could possibly

be so important that my name had to be

broadcast like that. I was surely going to

find out. I thanked the staff for the food and

began heading back down the hallway when

the EMT's rolled the deceased body into the

Yield

emergency room. Then I saw approximately five South Carolina State Troopers gathering in one of the exam rooms, talking to one of their own. I wanted to know more, even delaying the suspense as to why I was being paged. I needed to get in that room, but how I thought? Yes, yes, I'll pretend that I need to get the blood pressure cuff off the wall. I approached the exam room quietly then I knocked and said, excuse me I just need to get a piece of equipment that's right behind you sir. The trooper sitting on the bed looked towards me and said no problem ma'am and motion his hand for me to enter. Another trooper made a comment to him,

Yield

saying "don't worry, you will have a time to write your report".

As I exit, I looked at the trooper's facial expression as he sat on the bed and quickly realized that something happened involving him, but I was puzzled because looking at his outer appearance, he didn't look like he had been involved in an accident, so I thought. Paramedics were rolling the unknown deceased male down the hallway heading towards the elevator. I figured why not kill two birds with the same stone. I waited until the body was signed over to the security officer and I followed them to the elevator. I wasn't out of place because the

Yield

hospital's protocol is when a person has

expired the hallways should be cleared of all

non-hospital personnel, therefore I was not

asked to leave. The sheet placed over of the

body was saturated with blood in the chest

area. As the gurney rolled over the threshold

to get on the elevator, the sheet slipped off

the right foot. I began to yield. Out of

nowhere, I started shaking, but I didn't

understand why. I'm used to seeing dead

bodies, blood, feces, vomit, etc. It was

something about that "shoe". I turned

towards the stairwell and out the door I

went. I wanted to see if I knew this young

man. So, I waited until his body was

transferred over to the cooling table (freezer)

Yield

and when the coast cleared, the security

officer allowed me to get a sneak peek. And

beyond my darkest hour, I was in total

disbelief! I don't even remember passing

out. The security officer got me out of there

very quickly. He kneeled beside me and

asked if I was okay. I couldn't speak at first.

He said, well do you know him? My head

felt heavy as I tried to nod. I let out a cry for

mercy saying yes, he's my son's father! He

helped me to my feet and I walked away

feeling completely emptied. All I could do

was picture Derrick's facial expression

which looked as if he was in pain. Near his

right eye appeared to look as if he had one

dried tear drop that scrolled down to his

Yield

earlobe. Every step I took I tried to guess what could have possibly happen, who could have done this? Why? Where? He wasn't a fighter. When I got back to my unit, the staff were standing around the nurse's station speaking softly. I was asked to take a seat and I just stated that I had to get home to my children. The nurse manager said please sit, I have something I must tell you. I continued to ignore all requests looking for my car keys and the whole time they were in my pocket.

One nurse grabbed me, and my manager said that someone would drive you home because an incident occurred, and it was

Yield

very serious. I heard her, but I couldn't feel anything. I needed a way out. I told her that I had to use the restroom and I would be right back. I managed to slip away and ran as fast as I could. Once outside, I could not think where my car was, and I even forgot what color it was. I had to collect my thoughts quickly before they found me. I found it, my car was parked three rows away. On the ride, back to my parents' house I tried to press replay, but nothing happened. I turned my radio up, but the sounds were mute. I saw Derrick's face in my rearview mirror and he was smiling, showing off his beautiful white teeth. Am I dreaming I thought? Could this really be

Yield

happening? Lord, I can't take no more.
When I arrived home, my mother met me
the door and asked me did I seen Derrick? I
thought why you are asking me this now ma.
She said, he ran out of the house so fast that
she didn't see which way he went. Now, I'm
totally lost and confused; ma what happened
here? Where are my kids? By this time my
baby boy came on the porch and I noticed
that his hands were wet. As I walked closer
to hug him I realized that his hands were
bleeding. I yelled out Oh Lord, my mother
was hysterical and screaming at the sight of
blood, Denise stop it and you got to go find
Derrick, its dark outside. I said ma, talk to
me what's going on. She stated that she was

Yield

taking a bath when the telephone rang and

the next thing she knew my oldest son was

screaming at the top of his lungs. She

jumped out of the tub, grabbed a towel and

ran towards the kitchen. My son was

jumping up and down saying that the lady

told him that a police officer shot and killed

his daddy. Then he ran out the door crying. I

couldn't fathom all that was happening. My

oldest son it out in the darkness alone

somewhere; my baby boy hands were

bleeding. His nerves were so bad after

learning that his dad was dead, he bit nearly

all the nail bed off causing them to bleed.

My daughter was sitting on the chair crying,

she was too young to understand the chaos

that was taking place. I knew that I had to
get my son some medical treatment asap. I
didn't waste another moment, I scooped
Darion up in my arms and told my mother to
get my daughter and before I could call the
police my brother and step dad was pulling
up in the driveway. I yelled out to them find
my baby! I'm going back to the hospital
with Darion.

The whole drive back I prayed that God
protect my son and let them find him soon
and for the lady who called my house and
told my nine-year-old such tragic news she
better prays that I never see her again. Upon
arrival, the staff already knew that the

Yield

deceased male was my son's father, so they treated my baby boy quickly and out the door we went. My brother found my son near the edge of the woods jabbing a stick into the ground crying and repeatedly saying, I hate the police, I hate the police! The next day after staying awake watching my babies tossing and crying in their sleep, I had to run some errands. I needed some fuel. I pulled up at the station and as I began to pump my gas a lady walked over to my car and said I'm so sorry to hear about your loss, how are the boys holding up? I started saying to her how things were and then it happened.... she interrupted me and said yeah, I was the one who call to tell your

Yield

momma about what happened to big Derrick and your son answered the phone. One thousand and six demons ran through my mind, body and soul and they were all cheering me on to spray some gas on her as she stood in front of me puffing on her cigarette. There were several other people at the station and the sound of my voice attracted one man who became a hero, saint, angel and a negotiator all at once. I was so angry; I cursed her for everything that I thought she was. Nothing else mattered, I wanted to make her life a living hell. The man said ma'am please don't do it, you're going to kill all of us and who would be there for your children. Please ma'am calm

Yield

down. He turned to her and said why in the hell are you still trying to make peace with the devil, just leave!

He took the nozzle away from me and placed it back on the pump. All I could do was sit in my car and cry. I was all out of words. I gathered myself enough to drive off; however, the rest of my errands were left undone. I went back to my children and got on my knees and promised them that I would never do anything that will take me away from them forever. We hugged and cried together. In the heat of passion, one doesn't stop to think that all it takes is a split second and a life can forevermore be

Yield

changed. I had to get on my knees and
begged God to not only hear my cry, but to
forgive me for allowing the devil to lead me
near the pits of hell. Back to trying to deal
with our lost we had many questions, but
only got a few of them answered. I went into
a denial phase. I allowed my pride to stand
before me, so I never sought treatment for
myself, but I sought the help for my young
children as they needed it. Still unable to
grasp *why*, I began to focus more on how I
was going to manage by being strong
because my children meant everything to
me. They knew that I had invested all my
time and energy into making life better for
them. As my children grew older, they too

Yield

acknowledged my hard work and
commitment to providing their basic needs
and giving a little extra when I could afford
to do so. Sounds familiar yet? Yes, a pattern
of what my parent gave me and my sibling
when I was a child. I was traveling on the
right path, but the road kept yielding to other
life changing events that kept me driving
slower, but steady pace.

Time heals all wounds, I met an Army
Reservist who appear to be an officer and a
gentleman. We dated for a year and a half
before he asked my step-dad for my hand in
marriage. We got married at my church on
my 22nd birthday. Our marriage lasted one

Yield

year, one week and five days. And three

months after we separated, he had his first-

born child. So, that should tell you why the

marriage didn't last. In the beginning, our

relationship got off to a great start. Although

he was in the military, he had an opportunity

to participate in the NFL tryouts in Seattle as

a walk on recruit. His reason for rejecting

such prestige offer was because he didn't

want to leave me. I tried to get him to

understand that if he went and made it our

lives would be changed forever. His mind

was set and so that golden chance was

missed. I was very disappointed because

who wouldn't want the finer things in life.

We moved passed that and without warning

Yield

I started noticing the difference in his behavior. He began screening my calls, showing up at my work place when he should have been on his job, and every time I wanted to go to the store or visit family members, he felt the need to be right there. So, with this happening I began to ask questions. My main question was what happened to the trust? Where did it go? He could never give me any clear reasons behind any of his bizarre actions. I told him if he did not get his act together than he would find his self by himself. I was not about to deal with his insecurities after we vowed before God to honor and obey one another. So, one night after I got off from

Yield

work I noticed that he was not home, so I began preparing to get settled in for the night. I called my mother to check on the kids because my work hours and their school schedule conflicted and honestly, she never wanted my children to leave her home. I was headed back down the hallway when I heard a noise. I stopped, looked around and listen. Nothing, so I thought maybe it was the air condition unit outside. I took a few more steps and then I heard it again, this time before I could turn around it happened....it felt like my life was slowly being drained out of me. I was going down to my knees, the hallway continued to darken. I thought about my children; I saw

Yield

the grief on my mother's face and that's

when all hell broke loose. I began to fight

for my life as I did when I was a little girl.

Only this time I had more strength and street

sense. I managed to turn my body to face

this intruder, but I couldn't see his face

because he wore a ski mask. I fought with

all that I had, and I kicked him right between

his legs and his hands loosen from around

my neck and I was literally running away on

my knees until I made it to my feet and I

dash out my front door as if I was running

the 100-yard dash. I made it to the store at

the corner, but it was closed. I used the pay

phone to call my brother. I told him that I

needed him to come and get me because the

Yield

house was on fire. Now you are probably
thinking why lie? Why didn't you dial 911?
All I can say is that if you have never been
in a situation like this than you would
probably never understand the actions one
does in a life threaten situation. I was
twenty-two, my brother lives approximately
fifteen minutes away I wanted him to protect
me like he uses to when I was young.

Meanwhile all this is happening in real time
and I looked down the road and saw him yes
him, my ex-husband walking in my
direction. He was telling me that he was
playing a joke on me and it was ok to come
back home. I was totally lost for words.

Yield

How could the man I married do this to me? I flagged down a car as it got closer and it stopped. It just so happened that the driver was a friend of the family and he allow me to get in his car and we drove away, and I called my brother back and told him the truth. Let's just say that God sent my guardian angel in the nick of time because had my brother pulled up and learned the truth as my husband was walking down the road things would have had a very different ending. The next day with an escort I went back to the home and started packing all my belongings and in the process, I found a letter written by my estranged husband in a box in the top of the closet saying how we

Yield

would always be together even after death. This marriage was over, and I believe what lead him to this point was because he decided to have an affair and the female became pregnant and he couldn't face telling me the truth or losing me once I found out.

Years have passed and now my children are young teenagers. I was thinking about making a change in my atmosphere. The boys made their voice heard that they wanted to stay in South Carolina and finished high school. So, I pushed that thought back into my long-term memory bank. God has brought me through some of the most challenging events that life had to offer me. The only way I would consider the thought of leaving my children behind a life or death situation would have to occur. I stood firm on my faith and trusted God to continue to provide for us. When things are going good, the devil will always find a way to try and bring you right back to that dark place.

My daughter was fifteen years old and she had one wish for her sweet sixteenth birthday. I tried explaining the concept to her again about the male companion that I thought was her biological father, but Deoxyribonucleic Acid (DNA) stated otherwise. I wasn't ashamed about the results because he had enlisted in the

military and I didn't rush the testing because

I knew he could be located. I was ashamed

because so many years had passed, and I

didn't act sooner. So, with this confirmation

I knew I had my work cut out for me again.

The good news was that I was certain who

her biological father was. I just needed help

locating him. I shared with her that he did

have the opportunity to see her in person

when she was only three years old. I knew

she wouldn't remember that, but it did make

her smile just for a few seconds. So, the

search was on again, my sisters did what

they could do to help me. In 2004, the extra

hard work had paid off; I located him!

Yield

Finding her father became a daily topic as the time passed by. So, when she would ask ma, any new leads yet? I would just tell her that things were looking good. I knew that waiting until her birthday in October was entirely too long. So, a few more months went by than her father and I made contact again. I told him let's go ahead and make this happen. He couldn't agree more. Although, I really wanted to honor her wish on her sixteenth birthday, but I couldn't take having the same question thrown at me over and over when I knew, I had the correct answer. Celebrating with family and enjoying the beautiful South went by so quickly. School was back in and it was time

Yield

for Lights, Cameras, and Action. She was about to get the shock of her life. On the date set for her to meet her father, she had cheerleading practice. So, as I sat in the school parking waiting on her, I thanked God again for allowing this union to occur. I was so excited for her and she had no clue and it wasn't even her birthday month. All I could think about was capturing the look on her face when she sees him for her very first time. My cell phone rang, and it was my dear sister who had worked so hard in helping make her niece one wish come true. Than it happened…. she said sis, have you heard? I replied, heard what? She said Boo-Boo is dead. I froze up on a hot sunny day,

Yield

my mouth dropped, it felt like my heart
stopped again and my eyes filled with tears,
but the initial shock overshadowed my
frozen body and it would not allow one tear
to fall. Suddenly, I snapped out of it and
replied; hell no, no, no…. he promised that
he would meet her. What am I going to do?
How do I tell her? Will she hate me because
of the time that has passed? I knew I was in
for a long night. I told my sister that I had to
go, and I would call her back later. I saw the
school resource officer sitting in his patrol
car in the parking lot, so I ran over to him
and informed him of the news that I just
received and that I had to tell my daughter
this, but I couldn't do it alone, would he be

Yield

there for me. He said no problem. Also,

there were approximately five football

players dressed out for practice standing

close by. I also recruited them for the

manpower that I knew I would need. They

all agreed to assist me. Moments later, my

daughter came out of the building and as she

approached my car, I felt that she sensed

something was wrong. She got in the car sat

down with a distinct look on her face and

asked ma, what's wrong? I told her to get in

and put her seatbelt on. Immediately, she

knew something wasn't right because I

hadn't even started the car yet. The football

players stood by carrying on a normal

conversation. The resource officer pulled a

Yield

little closer. I said to her that I had some good news and bad news to share with her. She immediately insinuated that I located her father and he didn't want to meet her. I replied, yes and no. I told her that her auntie Renee assisted me with locating her father and I spoke with him over the telephone recently and we were going to surprise her this weekend. But, I received a phone call a few minutes ago, stating that he was de....

I never got the complete word out of my mouth she began screaming, kicking and calling on the Lord. The football players reacted quickly as well as the resource officer. By this time, she was on the ground

Yield

just outside the car door hyperventilating.

EMS was dispatched to the school parking

lot. They treated her on the scene and got

her calm down and she was released in my

care. I didn't know how I was going to fix

this. The drive back to the house was

painstaking. I lost all hope again just that

quickly. How could everything be going so

good take a "U" turn like this? I thought the

passing of my son's father was rough, but

every time death comes tragically

unexpected it never gets any easier. I

questioned God and asked why me again

Lord? I couldn't take away my children

pain, I couldn't answer their questions. I

began to doubt myself as not being the best

Yield

role model. My life flashed before my eyes,
I was working full time, furthered my
education, and I had also served my country.
And I gave my children all of me. I just
wanted the hurt and suffering for them to
stop. The road just kept yielding in the
opposite direction. Here I am again driving
at a slower speed, but steady.

May 9, 2005, I captured that look on my
daughter's face. A lot of people thinks she
looks like me but when I see her I see her
father. She met her father for the first time at
the funeral home. She talked to him, she
rubbed his hands, she kissed his forehead,
she begged God to allow him to wake up

Yield

long enough for him to talk to her and then
he could go back to sleep. Is this dejavu?
Because I wanted my father to wake up and
speak to me. She repeatedly cried out
Daddy, I Love You! There was no turning
back. This sudden death was devastating.
She was numbed on the day of his funeral.
She wouldn't eat, she wouldn't speak, and
she just cried and cried. I needed family
support. My daughter slept in my beds for
days. I was already playing the role well of
being mommy/daddy to my sons. Now all
my children were fatherless! I knew that I
needed to allow his family to grieve in peace
before taking her to meet them. God is an
on-time although, I doubted him a few times

Yield

myself. Through the storms and all the rain, I knew that the sun will shine again. A little over two months, I contacted one of his sister's and she decided to listen to my story. That one call generated numerous telegram messages throughout his entire family in and out of state. God is still in control.

Once again, lights, camera, action! I set up a family meeting with as many family members that wanted to be a part of this special union. I withheld this information from my daughter until I got her to the location. I feared of something else going wrong that could have easily pushed me and her over the edge. My sister in law and my

Yield

cousin who had traveled from North
Carolina just to part take is this new
beginning for my daughter. We told her that
we were going to McDonald's to get some
ice cream. She wondered why she was
invited because we were the old crew. I told
her that it was an all-girls affair. She bought
it. Sitting inside McDonald's anxiously
awaiting on that one call trying to act normal
was nerve reckoning, this time I was looking
forward to hearing a cell phone ring. This
call was expected, and it came moments
later. My sister in law asked, if I would take
her by a local restaurant to check out the
venue because she was planning a surprise
birthday party for her mother. I agreed,

Yield

although I knew that was our cue that

everything was set in place. We drove away

from McDonald's and within minutes

arrived at our destination. My daughter

didn't have a clue as to what was about to

transpire. Karen asked for us to get out and

come inside to give our opinion about the

location. So, it was planned that my

daughter was last in line. As the doors

opened we were already in a single file line,

so we walked in and stood to the side and

when my daughter appeared in the doorway,

her father's family members were standing

in a semi-circle holding hands. One lady

began singing. My baby stopped dead in her

tracks. One of his aunt said, "Sha baby,

Yield

welcome to the family". She went down on her knees and cried tears of joy!

At this time, another family member entered the room from the kitchen area walking towards the front door and when she saw Sha's, face she started screaming: she looks like Booboo, she looks like Booboo, then she bolted to the back of the room knocking over chairs and scattering tables. Another family member ran and caught her, and he held her tight. She continued to cry out, Oh my God his back. It wasn't a dry eye in the room. Truthfully, here it is years later and every time I think about that special day, I still get emotional. Everyone embraced me,

Yield

my daughter and my family members that were in attendance with open arms. Sha received several items that belonged to her father including one of his favorite green shirts that he had put in the dry cleaners a day before his death. Today, those items are still hanging up in her closet. We sat and ate the meal that was prepared especially for us. Now that's genuine love. Since their union, my daughter has been able to fill that void with her father's family and she met her half brothers and sisters. I asked her one question I needed an answer too. Are you angry at me for the way things turned out with finding your dad? She looked at me and said ma, God doesn't make any mistakes. I must

Yield

continue to learn to accept the things that I can't change. And after meeting my family the way that I did, I would never forget that picture perfect moment. Just maybe, if my dad would have met me and spoiled me, I probably would have turned out differently. No ma, I'm not angry at you, I'm happy that you are my mother. Ma, I love you.

I felt relieved knowing that my daughter still loves me. Single parents let not your hearts be dismayed. Trouble may come in the night time, and trouble doesn't last always. Joy comes in the morning time. If you put forth the effort to making sure you are the

Yield

|provider and not the enabler for your

children good thing will happen. People will

always have something to say about you

regardless if its' positive or negative. Misery

loves company. Use your energy to build a

solid foundation that carries you through all

things that life possibly offers you. Know

your self-worth. Having children is not a

curse; it's a beautiful creation from God,

trust him. Love yourself every day. Yield to

the roads that lies ahead, don't make a

complete stop, just drive slower.

Don't stress about taking an alternative route,

you'll still get there!

Detour

After all that I had endured, I found someone who also had challenges they too had to overcome. I figured with our past behind us, we could take this journey together to reach the same destination. Unaware that this would be the one relationship that almost cost me my freedom. I looked up just in time to make a quick detour before I reached the last barrier that lie ahead.

Little that I knew he was the devil himself dressed in Prada. Not once did I look at his past and placed judgment upon him. Nearly, a year later his true colors were slowly revealing. He was on drugs and I didn't realize it until one Friday evening he had asked to borrow my car to go see his brother. I never saw my car again, because he sold it for

Detour

cocaine. He stumbles back upon my door steps
nearly six hours later giving me a fabricated story
that he was robbed at gun point. But God works in
mysterious ways because I had already received a
call stating that he was seen at the crack house.
When I truly realized that I was taken for a ride it
was almost too late. He had pawn nearly all my
jewelry, sold most of my sneakers and handbags
and my brand new 9mm handgun. I owned so many
pairs of sneakers and handbags I didn't realize any
of them missing. This relationship was over from
the start. I tried to move forward but the pain of
deceit wasn't allowing me to forget what he did. I
hated myself because I let him into my children's
lives, he wasn't a stranger to my family. How could
this be? So, I worked and worked trying to forget

Detour

this part of my life ever happened. I was
dumbfounded because I didn't know what the signs
were. He hid them very well. He was never
physically abusive, but his actions took a mental toll
on me. Then one night after getting off from work, I
walked outside of my job and noticed that my car
was missing from the parking lot. Immediately, I
called the police. I felt that he had something to do
with the disappearance of my vehicle. The next day,
when I arrived back at work, I received a call from
him stating my car was across the street if I wanted
it back. I notified that police again. When we got
over to my car, there was a hand-written note placed
underneath one of the wind shield wiper blades that
read Tick, Tick Boom! Immediately, the bomb
squad was called out to clear my vehicle, but

Detour

nothing was found, and I was advised to seek a restraining order against him. At this point, I knew I had to act quickly because my life and my children's lives depended on it. Somehow, I worked my shift knowing that legal actions were about to take place. I was picked up from work and I tried to make sense of all the things that he was continuously doing even though the relation was completely over. That same night when I arrived at my parent's house while pulling into the driveway a male subject came running from the open field with and object in his hands. It startled both of us. I recognized him…OMG! I tried to get out of the car and she grabbed my arm and yelled no he will try to kill you. I was furious, and the thought of death surely entered my mind, but I was certain that it

Detour

wasn't going to be me. No time to escape from her death grip, she quickly placed the car in reverse and began backing out of the driveway. When she turned her vehicle around we heard this loud clashing sound. He threw a brick into her was back windshield and it landed on the seat. I contacted the police and they met us a few blocks away from my parents' home. I gave the police all his pertinent information and a background check quickly revealed more hidden truth about him. He had served time in prison for the sales of illegal narcotics, attempted murder, kidnapping and a slew of other charges stemming from when he was only thirteen years old. I was disgusted! Given this guy's criminal history, the responding officers suited up and was prepared for the worst. The sergeant said,

Detour

ma'am this is for our safety because we are dealing
with a walking time bomb. I tried calling my
parents' house phone, but the line was busy. I just
knew that he had entered the residence and killed
my family. I was beside myself crying hysterically.
Life had no meaning if something had happened to
them. Now, some of you may ask has the devil
bought my soul yet. The answer is no, but I gave
him a down payment for a thirty-day money back
guaranteed deal because that was all I needed. I
knew that God was the ultimate decision maker; but
truth be told that night, I had determined that I
would be the one to take his last breath. Game
Over! Meanwhile, the police made their move, they
surrounded my parents' house with guns drawn. I
had to stay outside in a patrol car until the residence

Detour

was cleared. Those couple of minutes felt like hours. Finally, the sergeant approach me and said

ma'am, your family is safe, please come with me. This ordeal only added enormous stress and more questions to the unanswered list. Thank God, my children and my parents were unharmed. The next day, I went to the local police department and asked to speak with a judge. Once I walked into his office, I asked him if he wanted to read my letter or should I read it to him. He had a look of uncertainty because he was clueless as to my unexpected visit. My letter was my confession: premediated, before the fact of a felony. Because I promised myself if I ever laid eyes on him again, I was going to take his life in exchanged for all the grief and torment that

Detour

he caused me and my family especially after all that we have been through. The judge was taken aback by my words and called in a deputy and closed his office door. He said to me, young lady do you realize what you are saying? I replied, yes sir, with tears in my eyes; I said, I am in my right mind and this letter was written by my own free will without any form of duress or coercion. Because he knew my family he tried to get to the bottom of my despair. I explained to him the actions leading up to that day taken by the man who betrayed my trust and jeopardized the safety of my family. And I would be dammed if I allowed any more pain or harm come towards the ones that I cherish the most. After carefully consideration, with a heart to heart talk with the judge listening to my cry for justice; I

Detour

was given a chance to keep my freedom by walking out of the building. There is a God who sits high and looks low. It doesn't matter what the form of abuse is, it is never ok but until you (victim) has reached the point of no return it will continue. The question then becomes is your life worth living? Yes, it is. So, take away their power by breaking the silence. I personally tried to overcome one obstacle after another on my own. I was only faced with more hurt and more added pressure placed upon me. In the past, I questioned God a few times, even though he has brought me through it, I'm still not certain if I really understand why. Things that are not clear often were design that way because if life was very straight forward than we would not have anything to look back on.

Detour

My life was filled with many different signs posted
along the roadways. My parent's health issues, me
almost missing out on my high school graduation,
losing my biological father, losing my niece and a
dear friend, teen pregnancy, losing my children's
fathers at such a young age, and being in an
unhealthy relationship. The journey that I'm on has
not been easy but I refuse to stop; so, I decided to
reset my GPS to finding faith and forgiveness and
continuing to drive on. I had to change my scenery
because my life at this stage was at the lowest point
on the chart. So, that long term memory of changing
my atmosphere suddenly reappeared. Regardless to
how far I traveled the devil was willing to continue
to work double time to recruit me. My parents knew
that if I didn't leave South Carolina to regain a fresh

Detour

start that the devil would defeat me. A family meeting was held and we all agreed that I should start over in a brand-new state. My friend came to my rescue.

November 1999, I set out to begin my new journey. That twenty-three-hour bus ride gave me ample time to reflect over my past, the what if's and what's next. I cried, slept, ate, prayed, cried and slept some more. I was happy and sad at the same time. This was my first time in this new state and I left me children behind with my parents until I could get settled with a place to call home for them. I knew I was on a mission that appeared almost impossible. No one moves to Vermont and find housing just like that especially during the winter

Detour

time. So, my mind was mapping out the things I
knew I had to do over the next few days. I arrived at
the Greyhound bus terminal in Burlington, Vermont
shortly after noon. The snow was beautiful, but I
didn't like wearing it up to my waist line. My friend
and her husband greeted me with a warm welcome.
I saw my luggage and as I am walking towards it
this older white woman stepped directly into my
pathway and asked me what I was doing there. It
was cold, and the wind was calm so maybe my
brain was frozen from the high levels of snow. I
said excuse me, she repeated her question this time
with a cattier tone. She said, I said, "what are you
doing here?" I began to smile looking her straight in
the eyes as I replied; "I'm here for the same reason
why you won't leave here, ma'am you have a

Detour

blessed day". I picked up my luggage turned and walked away. I could still see her out of the corner of my eye, she did not comprehend how I reversed her negative energy back onto her and kept my head held high maintaining my positive attitude.

Vermont is predominately a white state and blacks weren't very well accepted during this time. I'm not certain if much has changed. I felt that I would have a few more encounters like this one, but I wasn't about to allow someone else's words to redirect my determination. It's never about what a person says to you or about you, it's how you respond and or react to the situation which will define the person you really are.

Detour

We had a good Thanksgiving holiday. I spend
ample time on the telephone with my children and
my parents. That following week was show time. I
enrolled in the community college and I got a job
working as a telemarketer. It wasn't the best job,
but hey the pay was cool, and I got to interact with
others, so hours went by fast. Hearing to my
communication skills on the telephone, I was often
mistaken for a white girl. Most times, the person on
the opposite end of the call was taken aback, but
they appreciated me as a professional
representative. I wouldn't have asked for it any
other more. That evening, I got on the bus, I paid
my fare and sat near to front. The driver was very
nice; he could tell that I was a visitor or just moved
here. Back then, that's how many black people lived

Detour

in Vermont. This experienced opened my eyes to how we as people are still so divided in our country.

Each day that past, I promised myself that I would learn something new and retain it. The Community College of Vermont wasn't challenging enough for me. Seriously, I felt like I was back in high school. It appeared that everything was made easy for the citizens living here. After a year at the community college, I transferred to Burlington College and started working on my Bachelor of Arts degree in Human Services. I had some amazing instructors, they didn't' look at the color of my skin trying to define me. They treated me with respect. I guess you're wondering shouldn't they have done so anyway, well I brought charm, values, morals,

Detour

wisdom, knowledge, respect and just as equal my integrity. This wasn't a topic for debate. Days turned into weeks and weeks and before I knew it, my deadline had approached. I was down to a few places left to review or the chances of finding an apartment would almost be impossible. I arrived at this one specific location just minutes away from where my friend lived. It was nice with a unique twist to it. The owner and I spoke openly about life and personal goals. She was sold on renting the place to me. I thought my search was over it happened...the door opened and there stood a young black female with two small boys and a stroller. She asked, is this apartment still available for rent? I looked at the owner and glanced back at this young lady and replied, you're the young lady I

Detour

met on the bus the other day. She introduced herself and stated that she recently arrived in Vermont from New York and she was in search of a place for her and her two kids. My heart immediately went out to her small children. Its' cold outside and my children are in the South where it's nice and warm. Than my mind said, wait a minute, you need to find a place just as well. I looked towards the ceiling of the apartment and said God please let this owner rent this apartment to this family today. I turned and walked over to both ladies and before she could ask me anything, I said, ma'am please consider renting to this young lady and her children so that they can have a place to call home. I left the pair in the kitchen talking but the young lady stopped me at the doorway and said thank you! We exchanged

Detour

telephone numbers and I left. I was a bit confused

only for a mere moment, but to know that I helped a

stranger really felt good. Little that I was expected

on this same day, I gain a lifetime friendship just

priceless. Tia, you are my sister through Christ. It's

been nearly twenty years and our friendship has

drawn us closer spiritually and geographically. One

night my friend and I sat in her living room

discussing our short and long-term goals. She stated

that she always wanted to join the military and I

asked her what's stopping her. She replied, her

weight. She didn't think that she could lose the

weight to meet the standard entry requirements. I

made a promise to her. If she goes and sign up, I

would too. The bet was on. The next couple of days

went by and I still did not have a place to call home

Detour

yet, but we went to the Air National Guard base and spoke with a recruiter. A few days after that we were taking the ASVAB test. We both passed it with flying colors. Reality started to set in…did I just really do that? OMG! I called my parents' and told them that I had a better plan. They were eager to hear it. I told them that I was joining the Air National Guard. At first, my mother wasn't too thrilled, but my step dad was looking at the bigger picture. It didn't take long to convince her that I was doing the right thing. I prayed that night and asked God specifically to show me if that's the road I needed to be traveling on. The next day, I received a call from the recruiter stating that she could not get me a basic training date until the following year, but I could start working with the unit until my

Detour

orders came through. This was a full-time job being on orders. The only problem was that I still had not found a place to call home yet. I trusted that God was back in control over my life and I accepted the offer and that same day, I found a beautiful three-bedroom townhouse just minutes away from everything and right on the bus line. Lord, I thank you again, and again. My friend did not continue her military dream. She was very happy for me and became one of my biggest supporters. Things were really beginning to look up and moving quickly. For the first time in a long time, I had my life given back to me.

My children were very excited that I was joining the military and they were going to be reunited with me

Detour

very soon. Meanwhile, I served my country for four
years and received the Most Outstanding Airmen
Award during my basic training in San Antonio,
TX. In 2001, life was good. I brought my children
up to Vermont that summer and we had a grand ole
time. Although the boys weren't convinced to stay.
I was still a single parent, with stable income,
working towards my Bachelors' degree, having my
own place and now a member of the 158 Fighter
Wing was all like a dream come true. I was super
excited! I really started to like the new me.
Thanking God several times a day for his love,
guidance, patience, grace and mercy. Over the next
couple of years my youngest son began to seclude
himself more and more from his siblings and
cousins. My oldest called me and said mom

Detour

something is wrong with Darion. I thought who did something to my child. He said no ma, he just acts different from us. That didn't make me feel much better, but at least I knew that no one was trying to harm him. I spoke to my baby boy in length and he opened to me and said ma, yes, I'm different, I asked son how so? He said because I don't like girls, I like…. boys. I was speechless. I didn't see any signs besides the fact that he loved doing house chores, but all the other kids had house chores as well. My brothers did house chores when they were growing up too. I was taken by surprise because this was something new and I had no clue how to deal with this type of situation. One thing I knew for certain that he is my son and I was going to continue to love him unconditionally. I asked him to

Detour

help me better understand his emotions and
concerns. Little that I knew he had written a four-
page letter to inform me of his personal feelings
saying that if the family could not except him the
way he was than he would rather be dead or leave
us forever. I booked the next available flight out of
Burlington to Columbia, South Carolina and drove
directly to my parent's home. A family meeting was
held, and everyone's thoughts, feelings, concerns,
comments and questions were heard and answered,
but at the end of the night my family was still one
big happy family.

Reader's listen to me clearly. If you have a child or
children, a relative, and or know of someone whose
sexual preference is different from yours or what

Detour

you may consider is not the "norm" please yield

than stop and don't try to make a quick "u" turn, nor

should you take a detour away from them. I suggest

that you use caution as to how you approach an

individual because remember he or she is a human

being. There is only one Creator and that's God.

Despite what you think or know is right or wrong

don't judge anybody? You see, a sin is a sin

regardless of how big or how small it is. I can't get

any one of my children into Heaven, but faith and

forgiveness will. All the obstacles that I had come

face to face with throughout my life thus far and my

mindset for what I thought was right at that time to

do. God's timing, his will and his way will be done.

Some children often feel that no one is willing to

listen to them or stand in their corner when life

Detour

throws them a curve ball. Guess what parents,

teachers, preachers, doctors, lawyers, officers,

families and friends…. we are all on the same

playing field. God gives us so many chances to live

an abundant life. One should not deprive another

from the liberties that were already given to us.

When something good happens you often hear

people say, God is good all the time and all the time

God is good. So, when God creates a new life and

the doctor says it's a boy or girl, he doesn't follow

up by saying oh, this one is bad or that one is a

lesbian or he might be gay. A good mother will

stand by her children and continue to pray for them.

Darion is a high school graduate. He currently

resides in Atlanta Georgia; he works two jobs, he's

loved by many: family, heterosexuals, gays,

Detour

lesbians, and yes Christians. He has his own vehicle

a nice one might I add, and yes, he has good credit.

He has never been in any kind of trouble and yes, he

believes in God. My child is proud of who he is,

and I'm honored to be his mother. Darion, the love I

have for you as your mother is unbreakable! One

young man approached me and stated that he is gay,

and his mother is a pastor and she's ashamed of

him, so that's why he seldom travels to see her.

Whoever disowns God before others will be denied

before his father in Heaven. God said to love

everyone and judge no one. I knew that God was

still in charge of my life. I could accept the

information my son shared, but most importantly to

me as a mother, I help save my child's life!

Detour

My daughter knows all too well about life changing events. She was rushed to the emergency room for excessive bleeding. That evening we learned that she was pregnant with not one, nor two, but three individual sacs. The treating physician even had to take a seat on the chair as she further explained the ultrasounds. She was pregnant with triplets and one of the sacs appeared as if it could possibly divide again. We all were flabbergasted. I know that hearing I'm pregnant should be a joyous moment; but when you hear the words that I'm pregnant with triplets, my first thought was who was going to care for all them babies??? Once the initial shock wore off we regain our composure and began to listen to the information the doctor shared. My daughter only stood about five feet, four inches tall and three plus

Detour

babies would not be a good look on her. Early in her

pregnancy she was labeled as high risk and the

doctor placed her on bed rest. After several months,

she started having complications which lead to a

decision of saving her life or try to save the babies.

That was a no brainer for me, doctor do all that you

can to save my child. We anticipated having all

three, or four little one's nine months later but not

without their mother. Her white blood cells count

was nearly triple as to what it should have been.

Test were run to rule out many other health

concerns, but the thought of cancer was unbearable

by itself. My daughter was scared and confused at

the same time. I called Jesus on the main line again

and left him a voice mail. He didn't answer me

immediately because he was in the operating room,

Detour

and yes, her surgery was a success. We prayed together and cried together, but most importantly, we had to give our worries to the Lord. Once again, God is in control. There were many days that she experienced periods of depressed moments, but she managed to hold on to God's unchanging hands. As a mother, I know that she needed me more than ever. The love and compassion I had to offer her went hand in hand. I could not take away her pain, but I knew that with the love of our God earth has no sorrow that heaven can't heal. Time passed, and her faith never faded. On December 16, 2013, God blessed her with a beautiful little baby girl named Peyton E'moni Guinyard also known as Gammie's girl & my "Lil Saint". May her little brothers and sister Kaidon, Kai'son & Keriston continue to

Detour

watch over her from Heaven. God is the creator of all things. God gives it and he takes it away. He knows what's best for each one of us. And it's a time and place for everything. Despite holding on to sorrow-one should cherish the memories and believe that something greater will happen at the time in their lives when love seems hopeless and faith is nowhere to be found. A life changing event usually occurs for you to truly appreciate the power of God.

Start each day off with him and end each night with him. The love you have for your children should be a mere image of a greater love you share with God. Sometimes it's ok to be your child's best friend if it doesn't interfere with your parenting skills and or

Detour

the respect and morals that you have stored upon
them.

Start traveling on the road towards the Lord, renew
your faith and never walk by sight. Take the scenic
route if you want to get images in your mind as you
move about your journey. A picture may be worth a
thousand words, but faith without good works is
dead!

Many people have limitations therefore; everyone

should travel at a safe speed

45MPH

My granddaughter arrived just in time which gave
me a little over a month to spoil her before I headed
to the South Carolina Criminal Justice Academy for
the twelve-week basic law enforcement training
program. I don't know about you, but the only thing
that gets old on me are my clothes. At 43 years old,
I too want to continue to protect and serve my
community. I got off to a great start. I lost a couple
of pounds and added two shades of darkness to my
light caramel-slightly red complexion. My husband
was very proud of me. He became my motivator.
During my sixth week, my body had really taken a
beaten-by this time I had been mace, running &
jumping twisting & turning, falling, and fighting off
the bad guys. I knew that I was half way there and I
couldn't give up now. When we were given liberty

to leave, I went to Walgreens and purchase some icy hot because my body was sore, and my side was hurting nonstop. That evening right after my last training class, I felt a very sharp pain as if I was hit by a speeding bullet filled with salt and rubbing alcohol. I took a few steps and then it happened…. I collapsed to the pavement and thankfully my instructor was standing close by. He caught my head before it could hit the ground. I was rushed to Lexington Medical Center in Columbia, South Carolina. I laid in my tears and sweat in agony for hours. The Cadre had to call my county dispatch trying to reach my supervisor after all attempts made to the police department was unanswered. Dispatch advised the officers on duty over the scanner that someone needed to contact the academy because I was transported to the hospital.

My husband who was also a police officer was at

home in Beaufort and he was notified by his Chief

of police after he heard my name and the

information being released across the radio. Darryl

traveled to my parent's house pick them up and they

arrived just minutes after I was finally placed in a

treatment room. That's how long I waited to be

treated. A couple more hours went by and after all

the testing and x-rays, they couldn't find no kidney

stones or see any broken bones. Yet, I left highly

medication on one shot of morphine and several

prescriptions needing to be filled. Strain muscles &

muscle spasms together was a destructive

combination. My husband drove me back to the

academy that night. I couldn't go home because I

45MPH

had to finish out the week first. Besides we had a big test and I be dammed if I wanted to be recycled to sit and listen to those long lectures again. The next morning the captain was stunned to see me back. He called me in his office and said I'm sorry, but you can't be here. I looked as if nothing was wrong and said, but sir; I belong here. He appreciated my strength and determination but for my safety I had to leave. Ok I agreed, but not before this Friday I have this big test sir. He wasn't surprised that I countered him, but I placed him in a tough spot. He told me to go to class and let him think about it. When I entered my class, everyone was equally surprised after all, I was transported off the center by ambulance. He came to my class shortly after and said, ok this wasn't an easy

45MPH

decision, but do you think you can pass your test? I

replied, yes sir. He said are you sure because

judging from your appearance you look as if you're

still medicated and I need to know that you will be

able to clearly focus. I reassured him that I would

pass. Here it was only Wednesday, I'm sitting in the

back of the classroom smiling at everyone for no

reason. Yes, the morphine was still in full effect.

My roommate helped me get to and from class, to

our building and in and out of the cafeteria. This

struggle was real but again, I was not going to quit

now. The pain was steady, and the medication was

wearing down. I prayed and asked God to continue

to help me and to pick me up if I fall again. Prayer

does change things. I made it through Thursday and

thanking God for Friday. I passed my exam with an

45MPH

86 out of 100 percent and I gathered my belongings and slowly exit the building. I knew I had unfinished business and my return would be stronger than before. I was out for three weeks and returned on the April 19, 2014, the morning of my original graduation date. It was bitter-sweet, but I gained a new group of brothers & sisters and guess what, most of them were State Troopers cadets. I believed that everything that occurs happens for a reason. My son's father was killed by a state trooper and now I'm training side by side with a class full of them. I can't answer for that trooper back in 2005, but I know firsthand that all it takes is a split second to decide and either way it's one that you must live with for the rest of your life. So, in case you're still wondering, if I have any ill feelings

towards that trooper the answer is no because I
can't carry his burden regarding the choices he
made. I can only answer for my own actions. I
chose to become a certified policer officer to bring
about positive influence on my community and to
protect and serve all citizens. I chose to wear a
badge of honor, but I received my shield of
character directly from God. What's for me, will be
for. Time and time again, I had faced obstacles or
barriers but somehow; I was able to go around
them, over them, straight them or under them and as
low as I was I still managed to get right back up.

I returned at the South Carolina Criminal Justice
Academy to complete my final three weeks of

training. I received a voice mail from my daughter in law to call her as soon as I could. Immediately, my motherly instinct kicked in and my mind knew something was wrong and my stomach began to cramp. As I'm waiting on her to answer the phone, I thought he broke another limb while playing basketball again. She quickly clarified my curiosity which was the unthinkable. Derrick had a blood clot in his lung and he was in the Intensive Care Unit (ICU) in Germany. Fighting for another day, my son Derrick knows all too well about faith and our father's prayer. The next thing I know I was sitting in the office crying my tear ducts dry again. All I wanted was to get to my baby and hold him. God where are you, I shouted aloud. The staff tried to console me, but my world felt condemned and I

didn't have any room for comfort. Uncertain as to
what caused the clot he was being closely
monitored. As a mother who's so far away what can
I do? I need to get to my baby, but how? I didn't
have a passport readily available. I was in my tenth
week of training and if I leave now they would
understand the reason, but I would not successfully
complete and would have to start over. I was so
close to finishing. So, I went to my room and I
fought the devil, rebuking him and sent him back to
the pits of hell and then I consulted with God. I
opened my mind and my heart and prayed the
Lord's Prayer. I felt the spirit overcome my body
and entered my soul. By his stripes my child is
healed. I stopped worrying and gave it all over to
God and I asked him to give me a sign to let me

45MPH

know that my son will be alright. The next day, I

managed to regain my composure and honestly, I

slipped up and started worrying again. Now we

know that's not right, but if you trust and believe

that God will work it out give it to him and leave it

alone! Trying to help only hinders the amazing

miracles that he creates. The training day had come

to an end and as I walked out of the building, there

was a group of cadets standing around talking

among themselves. One guy stopped me and asked

if he could ask me a question. Well for the person

that I am, I said sure. He stated that on the day I

received my troubling news, he and some of his

classmates saw me running and crying. He added,

we don't know the extent of your worries but seeing

you in tears lead us to offer what we can do for you

today. They joined hands and encircled me, and he began to pray. All I could say was thank you, Lord. I know that no matter how long the healing process would take, that my son was going to be alright. I send a special thank you out to the Basic Jail training class **#338** of the South Carolina Criminal Justice Academy along with the administration staff and the instructors for their prayers, kind words of comfort and keeping me grounded to successfully complete this twelve-week challenge. It's been a couple of months now and my son is still on the road to recovery; but by God's grace and his mercy my baby is still alive. My granddaughter London said that she will take care of her daddy and for her mee-maw not to worry.

45MPH

Families usually come together when tragedy strikes. Some come with sympathy or empathy and others come simply to be noisy. In any given situation, someone maybe going through a breakthrough, family should always stand together in good times and in bad times. That's why having an intimate relationship with God; you will never have to struggle and carry the burden to fight a battle that you can't win on your own. I may not be a Trooper; but I am a soldier in the eyes of the Lord! On May 9, 2014, I received my badge of honor. I understand God's words. I live by his words. I worship and give praise to his words. Prayer is so powerful; use it as your single weapon to defeat the enemies in your neighborhood, in the community, in the workplace and in schools. His words are holy, saved and sanctified. They are the

foundation to building a stairway to heaven. Jesus

said that he would never mislead you nor forsake

you. It doesn't matter what road you're currently

traveling on; he can guide your direction from

where ever you are....so will you trust him?

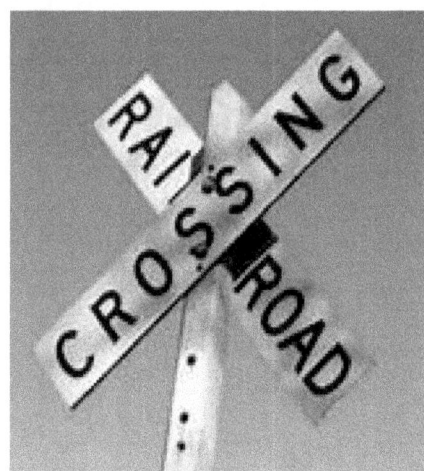

Be patient because eventually, you will cross over!

Railroad

I made it over the humps. I'm ready for what the world has to offer me. On May 21, 2005, I earned my Bachelor of Arts in Human Services from Burlington College of Vermont. I crossed off another item on my bucket list. Graduating from college should be on everyone's wish list even though sometimes life changing events occur that prohibits one from accomplishing this goal. I encourage each one of you to dream big. My four years wasn't easy and many of times I wanted to quit, but my children were at the center of my heart and that's what kept me focus and driving on.

I had a lawsuit which settled out of court, but not before I had the opportunity to see the female driver who continued to show no respect for others specifically, black people. She sat across from me during her deposition and every chance she got, she exploited the "N" word, also calling me a monkey. My attorney had worn me that she probably would behave in this matter; but instead of me showing any emotions, I just sat there and allow her to make a complete fool of herself. Because of her outlandish choice of words, I *capitalized* on my case. I wondered if she ever ate bananas. I could relocate back to South Carolina safely with much more than what I had anticipated on having. Crossing the railroad tracks, please slow down or better yet come to a complete stop even if there is not a stop sign. Look in all directions for any traffic approaching or obstacles that could interfere with you crossing safely. Some tracks are worn out which makes them very uncomfortable to cross. I've only walked the tracks once in my life as a teenager and with every step it seems as if the tracks would never end nor could I see where it would lead me too. These tracks were made from iron and steel subject to very high stresses of constant travel. And we humans are made from pure love from our Heavenly Father and the stresses that are placed on our lives are there because we attempt to fix problems that are often out of our control.

Thinking back about all the railroad tracks I've crossed that has caused friction with the bumps and jilts, some rougher than others but after clearing the tracks, I realized that they were just obstacles that I've faced and overcome. God is the conductor of

45MPH

the train that I decided to aboard and ride along

life's journey therefore, I invite you to seek him as

your personal conductor as well!

God brought you to it, he will bring you

through it just have Faith!

Dead End

I had just finished my first draft, my degree project after long hours of nonstop typing. Now it was time to head back home to get some much-needed sleep so that I would be rejuvenated in time for my nine o'clock morning class. I called for a cab and waited. Twenty minutes had gone by, so I called again. I didn't think much of it because the services were usually slow; but that night not too many people were out stirring around.

Nearly fifteen more minutes had passed, and the cab appeared. I was so tired I didn't have the energy to ask the reason for the delay. I stated my address in Winooski and then she drove off. Minutes into the drive I notice that the driver was driving a little too fast within the city limits, so I tapped on the back of

Dead End

the driver seat and said, excuse me ma'am I would

appreciated it if you slow down my house is just a

few blocks away. She never said anything, but she

continued drinking out of a supersize cup that had

McDonald's logo on it. The cab began to drift off to

the right side of the road. I leaned forward and

tapped her on her right shoulder and repeated my

statement I made earlier. This time, my tone was

more demanding. Now, my fight or flight instinct

kicked in because I sensed that something was not

right. As we approached my street I was thankful to

see my apartment building. I placed my hand on the

door lash and then it happened......the driver head

went down as she leaned forward and the cab

picked up speed and within a flash, I screamed out

oh God no, oh God! Right when I thought it was

Dead End

safe to cross the railroad track it happened….at the blink of an eye, I was rolling out of the car into the middle of the roadway. Shock is an understatement to say the least. My final degree project was scattered all about the road. My mind could not even process fast enough what was happening to me. My career and the ability to live a normal & healthy life have reached a dead end. The cab ran into a crosswalk signed and then into my apartment building. The impact forced my hand to pull the latch and I fell out of the cab into the middle of the roadway and my papers were flying around like confetti being thrown around just as the ball drops down at Times Square on New Year's Day. One vehicle was approaching the traffic light and came to my aide. Emergency services were contacted, and

Dead End

the police were called. The driver was awake after
the crashed and she began raring the gas pedal
trying to get the cab off the crosswalk sign and out
of the apartment living room. I was transported to
the hospital because my head met the pavement in
an unpleasant way. I also had some minor scrapes &
bruises to my arms and hands. I called the police
department to report incident. I was released that
same night highly medicated on Percocet; but I was
determined to make it to school despite the pain I
was feeling; so that I could reprint my papers and
turn it in on time. I found out the next day that the
female cab driver that left the scene was
apprehended a short distance away from the
accident and arrested for driving under the
influence, driving without a driver's license and

Dead End

leaving the scene of an accident. This specific cab
company contacted me and made an offer of
$3000.00 for medical treatment and any
inconvenience. Listen, I didn't need a college
degree to know that this offer wouldn't even pay for
the short ambulance ride to the hospital. I kindly
declined the offer and sought legal advice. I prayed
about this matter to God because here I was a black
woman living in a predominantly white state my
chances of getting what I truly deserve would
probably take a miracle. I did my research and
found a law firm that was honored to accept my
case. It was clear that this lawyer had a bitter taste
in his mouth with this specific cab company from
many years ago. And now it was time to make them
put their money where their mouths were. I received

Dead End

months of physical therapy and chiropractic visits. I tried every thinkable home remedy to stop the pain in my head and neck. Hours and days went by and I remain feeling as though I was isolated from the rest of the world. If I went out during sunlight my eyes felt like an old furnace burning, my head felt as though a seasoned trucker driver decided to park his eighteen-wheeler on top of it for an entire summer vacation.

What is it for a girl to do? I'm taking the meds as prescribed and going to my appointments as scheduled yet still no relief. My future relied on me being in class for this final semester to orally present my degree project. Here I am all alone in a state with no family, but my friend and a few

Dead End

associates that I've befriended along the way. I can't face my family just yet because I have not obtained what I came here for. My children were depending on me. My parents looked up to me because I was their first child to go to college. I said to myself, Lord I'm so close but this pain is keeping me from reaching out and grabbing it. I stayed indoors unless it was a must that I go out. I began to cry and cry and cry until my tear ducts ran dry and my eyes began to hurt. At this point in my life there was *nothing* that I could do to fix this. I was not in control. I began blaming myself for this chapter in my life. Than it happened.... I began to substitute my trust for anything goes and my determination for destruction. My appetite was cut less than half. I began to crawl around my apartment because

Dead End

standing up made me feel nauseated. Many nights, I

slept on my bathroom floor due to the side effects of

the pain medications. I avoided looking in the

mirror because the reflection of light bounced off

the mirror straight into my eyes causing my head to

pound harder and harder. Living alone eighteen

hundred miles away from home, battling this

ongoing pain, I felt as though I had no identity. I

had to get and extension on my assignment because

I was unable to meet all the required deadlines.

Despite my personal feeling, I had to deal with

being harassed via telephone calls weekly from the

cab company still trying to make a deal with me

until my attorney put a stop to it. Well one would

think that all forms of harassment would cease; try

again, someone redefined an old slavery tactic and

Dead End

decided to place a drawing of a stick figure image with a rope around the neck with the word "nigger" written in black capitalized letters. And for the first time in my life I experience total hatred. All my trials & tribulations in the past didn't prepare me for this one. I knew that things were heading in the wrong direction, so I called my doctor and told him what I was experiencing. And without hesitation, he replied, get through tonight and I'll see you in my office at 9:00 o'clock. I managed to get through the long cold night; and with little to no sleep; I forced myself to get dressed and out the house. I took the transit to my appointment dressed in all dark clothing with a pair of dark shades and my hat & scarf set on. My dark colors weren't to disguise myself from being noticed, it was just the dark place

Dead End

I was in during this period of my life. I was feeling
as if I didn't belong anywhere anymore. The sounds
of laughter and others being jovial made me
cringed. I used to have that kind of life; but I had no
clue what happened to it. I even tried to fool myself
thinking that this doctor will be able to fix my
problems by changing my medications. The doctor
prescribed me something new that was less
sensitive to my stomach. I walked in the treatment
room and he said good morning, I'm so happy to
see you, then he reached out and touched my
shoulder. He added, well I've reviewed your chart
and noticed that you've had a lot going on over the
past few years; but I have one question for you. I
looked as though, I didn't have any more answers to
give and if I did I wouldn't be here now. The doctor

Dead End

asked, have you ever received counseling? I said no

sir, I'm not crazy, I…. he kindly interrupted and

said Crystal seeking counseling does not indicate

that a person is crazy; it simply means that

individual's sometimes need professional guidance

to help them overcome personal challenges that

interferes with their health and or social well-being.

These types of feeling and emotions are commonly

associated with a mental illness called: **Depression**.

I sat motionless, emptied, embarrassed and cold.
He continued rambling on, but the words sounded
as if he was speaking in another language. I tried to
wrap my mind around anything that would allow
me to escape from listening to this information. I
came up with nothing. I guess this was still the
denial phase that I held onto to for years. I looked at
the doctor and said please sir, help me get my life
back. I'll go where ever you send me. I left the
center with a new prescription, a referral to see a
professional counselor and the option to live to fight

another day. The ride back home gave me time to focus my attention on this unspeakable act directed towards me the day before.

I decided to tell my parents just in case anything should have happened to me they would have something to go on. They wanted me home no questions asked. I promise that I was coming back home but not until I graduate and see my lawsuit to the end. I had to trust God and stand on his holy word. If I start to run again I won't be ashamed because the course I'm traveling on; I'll only fear God.

Many people have occasional bouts of depression over their lifetime which is usually brought on by a specific situation or major life event. Per the Center of Disease Control depression is more prevalent in some southern states Honestly, I don't know how they skipped South Carolina. Depression rates vary by gender, age, and ethnicity.

One out of ten adults are stated to have reported depression and women are at higher risk of depression than men, ethnic minorities are at greater risk of depression than non-Hispanic whites, and adults aged 45-64 are more likely than any other age group to have a diagnosis of depression. Feeling sad or being mad doesn't mean that you have depression. If your symptoms continue longer than two weeks, I personally suggest that you seek professional advice.

Traveling in a circle may take you aback; just keeping going!

Circular Intersection Ahead

I look forward to waking up every morning, thanking God for blessing me and preparing me to start a new day off with joy in my heart and a smile on my face. On May 21, 2015, I went to work blessed and highly favored as usual. This day was like any other day with an agenda filled with meetings, scheduling appointments, seeing client's and of course lots of paperwork to process. Good morning, I said to my coworker's as I passed them in the hallway. I made it to my office and placed my purse in the second desk drawer along with my car keys. I turned on my computer and sat patiently thinking to myself today is going to be a great day in South Carolina. At approximately 9:13am, there was a knock at my office door and I said, "come in" the door opened, and the County Director was standing in the doorway staring at me with a smile on her face, looking so bright and she said "Denise, God spoke to me this morning, and he told me to tell you to slow down. Since you've been here you have been working in full speed. I don't want you to get burned out   and leave because you're not taking care of yourself. Have you taken your medicine this I morning?"   I replied, "yes ma'am." She said ok, I love you and she shut my door.

Now I don't know about any of you that's reading my book, but let's be honest. Have any of your supervisor's, team leaders, directors, presidents, etc. ever tell you that they love you from a spiritual perspective?   Probably not, I felt special and honored, I remembered looking up toward my ceiling saying, "thank you, Lord for sending an "*Angel*" to watch over me." Here it's now 9:26am and I was typing away than the fingers on my right hand began to feel tight. Mentally, I ignored it simply because it was early morning and I just assumed that my body was still waking up, although I felt fine. My eyes were constantly watching the clock on my radio because I had an appointment to meet with a client at 11am. Here it's now 9:48am and my right hand feels like it's getting tighter with the least kind of movement. I tried to shake it off, but no change. So, I got up from my desk and left my office. I went and asked a coworker if she had any Tylenol, but she didn't have anything to offer me. My Director was sitting in her office down the hall, around the corner and partially down another hallway and amazingly

Circular Intersection Ahead

she heard me asking for Tylenol. She asked aloud, "Denise what do you need Tylenol for"? I stood still in my tracks because I was in awe trying to figure out how in the world did she hear me asking for Tylenol? I began walking towards her office saying, it's okay I'm not in any pain but my hand and fingers are kind of weird. When I reached her office door some of my fingers were nearly stuck in a fixed position. Immediately, my Director said, "go and have that checked out right now". She added, do you need me to go with you? I replied, "no ma'am it's probably just a pinch nerve or something". She said please go and let me know if you need me, I will come to you. I thanked her, and said, I'll be fine. I must get to my 11am appointment first. I went back to my office sat down and tried to type again no use, so I picked up a

Circular Intersection Ahead

pen to sign a document and I was unable to grip the pen. I gave up, I shut down the computer got my purse and keys turned off my lights and locked my office door. As I was walking down the hall I yelled out to my Director ok I'm leaving now, she thought I had already left so she said again if you need me call me. I got in my car and drove approximately three miles to the Family Health Center in St. Matthews South Carolina. I pulled up in the parking lot and went to put my car in park trying to use my right hand, but my hand kept slipping off the gear handle. I reached over with my left hand and place the car in park. I got out and secured my vehicle and walked inside. The receptionist was sitting at the front desk waiting to greet me with a smile and a little bit of her Southern Hospitality.

Circular Intersection Ahead

I smiled back and asked if it was possible that I could have my blood pressure checked. There were no patients seated in the waiting room. I stated that I felt fine, but my right hand was feeling funny and tight. I looked down and noticed that my right arm felt like it was weighted down with blocks. I continued to ask for assistance, but I kept my eyes on my arm. The receptionist asked had I ever been seen their before and I told her no, I than realized OMG, I didn't have my insurance card in the purse I was carrying that day. Standing with my right hand and arm now feeling like somebody rubbed it down with Lidocaine cream, Orajel and Anbesol. I began explaining to her my situation as to why I did not have my insurance card and telling her who I was and where I worked, and that I would pay for their services if only I could get my blood pressure checked. For a quick second, I sounded like Tina Turner when she left Ike and ran to a hotel without any money, but because of her fame she was treated like a queen for a night. Back to my reality, I thought to myself what could this be? I than said Ms. ma'am I think I'm having stroke like symptoms. The nurse practitioner stuck her head from behind an opened door so quickly, she startled me. She replied, Miss.... did you say that you are having stroke like symptoms? I said, yes ma'am she said please come on back. So, I took one step and it felt like I was stepping down in the middle of an ocean. The nurse practitioner came to my aid and assisted me back to their triage room. Once I was seated I began telling them that I felt good except for my right hand and arm and now my right leg and at the bottom of my right foot was tingling. The more I talk I began to my words were not clear. My lip started itching by this time the reading of my blood pressure was **226/116**. The nurse practitioner had already started the F.A.S.T exam. This quick exam can help an individual get the proper medical treatment that could save their life.

1. **F** is the facial dropping check to see if one side of the face droops or is numb ask the person to smile.

2. **A** is the arm weakness check to see if one arm is weak or numb. Ask the person to raise both of their arm. Does one arm drifts downward?

3. **S** is to check their speech, is the person unable to speak? Is their speech slurred? Are they hard to understand? Ask them to repeat a simple sentence like: the sky is blue.

4. Time to call *911*. **If a person shows any of these symptoms even they go away call 911 and get them to a hospital immediately!!**

The next thing I knew the Director was contacted and she came over, they were trying to reach my husband by telephone, but no answer. Someone called the Sheriff's office and they tried contacting my husband still no answer, so the County Director drove to my residence and woke my husband to notify him in person. Meanwhile, it dawned on me that I was having a stroke. EMS personnel arrived and got me in the back of the ambulance very rapidly. At 10:14am I was being transported to the Regional

Circular Intersection Ahead

Medical Center in Orangeburg South Carolina. I remember saying aloud Lord I don't know the day and time that I will leave this world, but I want to remember the day and time that I came into this world. June 20, 1970 at 1:14am. I kept repeating it all to the hospital. I closed my eyes and began to pray for my husband, our parents, our children, our grandchildren, my siblings, my clients and my one sister that I have not spoken with in a long time. Than it happened…. the sounds of calmness became extremely chaotic. I saw men and women moving around like they were running late for work and its' their first day on the job. Questions were coming at me from all over the room I stopped looking around because trying to see who was talking directly at me

Circular Intersection Ahead

was making me dizzy. I thought I was answering their questions but apparently, they could not hear me, my blood sugar had dropped very low and I was not talking aloud. I needed medication to bring my blood sugar back up. Moments later, they could hear me again. What had appeared to be minutes to me was almost an hour. As I laid with my eyes glaring into the light in ceiling directly over my bed, I told God that I give myself back to him so that he can use me for his greater. I had no worries, nor did I feel any pain. A loud shout of my name being called guided my attention to the monitor screen in front of me. It was the stroke specialist team via satellite sitting in from The Medical University of Charleston hospital. Ms. Williams the voice spoke can you hear me? I answered yes ma'am, she than asked are you feeling pain anywhere? I answered no ma'am? She asked are you sure? I said yes ma'am. She scratched her head and ordered another CT scan. Another doctor stepped closer to my hospital bed and asked can you see how many fingers I'm holding up? At first my vision in my right eye was blurred upon arrival however; I could see his two fingers. My bottom lip was still slightly twisted, and I had been drooling on myself, but I knew they understood me. I was completely weak on my entire right side. I looked over and the Director was standing at the left side of my bed, I began to cry. She stated, "Don't you start that, listen to me God is in control and he's going to take care of you".

Circular Intersection Ahead

She started praising God as she stood there, saying thank you Jesus, she didn't have a stroke. The technician that was trying to start my IV looked over at her and said umm ma'am, she did have a stroke. The technician than asked are you a family member? She replied, this is my employee and she is also my sister through Christ. As the tears rolled down my face I looked over to my right and I saw my husband, who stood in disbelief hearing that his young beautiful wife had a stroke.

Looking through his eyes, I could see a wrinkle in his heart since he was lost for words because the air was knocked right out of him. I placed my hand over my heart and applied a little pressure to it giving him back the air that he had lost. Together we are *one*

Circular Intersection Ahead

heartbeat. Over the course of the day, I had gone through a battery of test: X-rays, an ultrasound of my Carotid Arteries, CT scan, MRI, EEG, EKG, just to name a few. Here I am at the age forty-five and look physically healthy, even my Hypertension can be manageable, yet it can still be a silent killer. That evening the news had spread like wild fire out in the forest in California. The countless prayers, thoughts, and financial support, displayed one of God's greatest gifts-love. All acts of kindness were graciously appreciated. That night when my family left, and my husband went home to gets some of my personal belongings, I quietly dosed off to sleep. My mind, was clear and my heart was content because I gave everything to Jesus and left it there. Not certain of the time, but I knew it was late within the midnight hours, a voice whispered in my right ear. The message was: "Hey cuz, its' me, Bobbie Ann. Don't worry you're going home tomorrow at 12 noon, I love you". I opened my eyes and looked around and saw no one standing there. I know it was her voice that I heard. I closed my eyes and said Lord, I'm ready to go wherever you lead me, I shall follow, whether it be at my house or in Heaven. I slept peacefully. The next morning, God allow me to see another day here on earth only meant one thing, my work here isn't done. I spent several days in the hospital roomed near the nurse's station. The former Chief of Springfield Police Department and his former Deputy Chief came to the hospital to visit me. They brought me flowers, balloons and most importantly the Chief personally hand delivered me my uniform. He wanted to assure me that my law enforcement career would be waiting on me once I was able to return. On May 4, 2015, I made history is Springfield, South Carolina being the **first** female ever to become a certified police officer; however, my stroke delayed my start date. All that happened throughout the day and night despite what the test results revealed, the doctor came into my room making his morning rounds and looked at me turned and he walked right back out of the room. A few minutes later he returned, his eyes were opened so wide if he stretched them any further his eyes would have fallen out. The doctor said, Mrs. Williams how are you feeling this morning? I responded, good sir, I'm ready to go home today. He conducted his little exams and discovered what everyone else already

Circular Intersection Ahead

knew that I had weakness on my right side. He then recommended that I start physical therapy.

So, the question became do you want to stay in the hospital or go the physical therapy as an outpatient? I replied, I'm ready to go home. He said, I understand but we need to run some more test to check to see if there are any new changes. He also said, this is new for him. I asked him did he just graduate for med school? He replied, no ma'am, after carefully reviewing all your test results from yesterday, I must admit that I am very surprised that you're not in the intensive care unit. I told him I can relate to him feeling that way because on yesterday when I gave my life back to Christ, he renewed my mind, body and soul, therefore; yesterday was my trial, today is my testimony, and tomorrow will be my triumph because God made it that way.

The doctor nodded his head and extended his hand and said continue doing what you're doing, and I should make a full recovery. At 11:58am, I was rolling down the hallway in a wheelchair waving to the nursing staff. They were all astound by my departure compared to my arrival. My husband was humbled to know that not only was I heading home; but that God gave me another chance to continue to live a normal life. However; my choice of foods would be carefully screened. I began to feel a little nervous during the ride back home because I had limited use of my right side and I was concerned about falling. However, I must say that my husband

Circular Intersection Ahead

and my children were **All-IN** with assisting me with
the things I never thought I would need their help
with. Something as simple as squeezing a small thin
wash cloth was challenging for me. There were times
that I cried when I was home alone. Honestly, I had
mix emotions: sometimes I was praising God for all
that he had done for me and sometimes I allow the
devil to control my most inner thoughts that I knew
God should have been the only person to know what
I was feeling. As weak as I was, I decided to take a
stand and trust God because I recalled as I was
leaving the hospital; I could see inside of a couple of
patient's rooms and they were lying on their backs,
in their beds with tubes and machines around them,
probably not even knowing where they were; but the
eye opener was not seeing any family members in

their rooms at that time it really brought me back to being grateful and I immediately began asking for forgiveness. That moment I decided to ask God to accept me again. My tongue had confessed my sins and my heart accepted Jesus Christ as my Lord and Savior. I gave myself back to him to use me as he saw fit because **"I"** alone am nothing! Rightfully owed, I want to give a very special thank you to the following: Mayor of Springfield, a church Pastor of Springfield, South Carolina, the Holly Hill Police Department, Chief Magistrate Judge of Orangeburg, South Carolina, Deputies of Orangeburg & Calhoun Counties, Pastor of New Faith Community Church, Pastor **Ronald Johnson** of Faith & Victory Outreach Ministries of Santee,

Circular Intersection Ahead

South Carolina, **Reverend CJ Way** of Mt. Hebron Baptist Church of Santee, Department of Social Services employees of Aiken & Orangeburg Counties, Family Health Center of St. Matthews, South Carolina and to my family and friends especially my sister, ***Ms. Tamalia Gidron*** of Columbia, South Carolina.

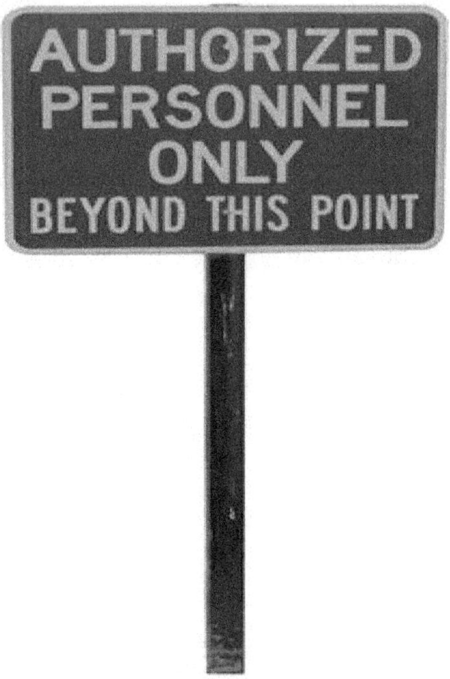
AUTHORIZED
PERSONNEL
ONLY
BEYOND THIS POINT

I surrendered All!

Authorized Personnel Only

Hopefully, you are starting to feel a bit more relax and have decided to let your hair down. Let the fresh air that God sends through your window cleanse your mind. I noticed that you are driving under the speed limit-it's okay, God will not allow you to go any faster than he really wants you too. Although, you are sitting in the driver's seat, he has full control of the wheel, so you are safe now, how awesome is that?

See some people fail to realize that their actions are not because that's how they made it to be...it's because the Almighty has allowed it to happen. When something good happens people often say, God is good all the time and all the time God is good! When a person dies, people often say God doesn't make any mistakes. So, when things aren't going well, and you call on him just know he is right there in the midst. Remember, you picked up FAITH along the highway when you were changing lanes.

Take a minute to reflect over your life up until now. You may have to stop at a few red lights to allow your past to catch up or you may see the yellow flashing light to caution you of something you are hesitant to reminisce about. Despite all those encounters, you still have a green light to "Go". Don't miss out on the life that God has chosen for you. Don't be afraid to show your love towards him. You have been feeling trapped inside of your own body, longing to be freed. All the hurts, lies, deceit, and tears needs a host to survive. Don't be fooled anymore, you are heading in the right direction. Didn't you know that when everything seems to be coming at you all at once…your blessing is near. Travel at a safe rate of speed but still be prepared to make sudden stops. Life's journey is mostly viewed as a straight road without any delays. If you haven't had any setbacks in your life than you would never understand a personal testimony of a comeback. You have the right of way to drive on at this point, keep looking ahead but also take time to view the scenery around you.

When Jesus says yes, it doesn't matter who said no! If you have a passenger, make sure they are seat belted in. Often, they too can cause a disruption along the path. Although you have a green light, still be observant of others. One that is envy will try any and everything to put obstacles in your way to keep you from reaching your destination. A female has a special order in the purpose of life. A woman created from a single rib of a man has a miraculous story to tell.

Although, the rib is strong and yet so delicate, the rib protects a man's heart and lungs that holds every breath that he takes. My faith in God, the father, the son and the Holy Spirit as made me an angel in God's eyes. I'm walking by faith and not by sight. On this journey that I travel daily, I'm not using a map on my road trips, only my God's Protective Shield (GPS). When you are happy, and things are going good you often say, Thank You, Lord.

When something happens, and we don't understand why, we say that only God knows best. When a sudden death occurs, or a horrific event happens especially to someone healthy and or young, people often say, God never makes any mistakes. And to those of us who have lost loved ones, we say everything happens for a reason. See the devil use to be an angel at one point in time, but because he chose greed over God's grace and gratitude he was cast out of heaven. Having faith doesn't require a diploma, certification nor a degree. All that's required is faith, the size of a mustard seed and God will bring you through your life experiences. Open your hearts and allow the love that was created deep within yourself to explode into the air affecting everyone you encounter. When and where there is love, there aren't any strangers because we are all God's children. Faith is the gateway to all blessings. Give all your doubts, troubles, worries, illnesses, addictions, bad habits, and fears to the Lord and leave it there.

If you've prayed about it, then don't worry about it anymore. It's just that simple when you have faith. I was reminded of this when my son was critically ill. My God, my God, oh how I love thee! I stretched my arms and extended my hands and he reached down and touched me. My son is better, and I say thank you to the medical team over in Germany. God was in the mist. Trust is not up for debate when you walk by faith. Sometimes, you may find yourself down and almost out stop, look around,

Authorized Personnel Only

and look up because God needs your undivided attention. This too shall pass. God can and will pick you up and place your feet back on stable ground. That's when your trial is over, so all you need to do is stand. Go ahead and free yourself from unhealthy stress, pay it forward and continue to pray about everything, but worry about nothing. He is still in charge.

Allow him to open doors in your life. God is an exquisite treasure piece, hold on to him because a real God-fearing man that enters your life is one of a kind. God holds the master key that will grant you complete entry to an all access pass to be productive and prosperous. Through his eyes, you are beautiful and worthy. Don't let anyone tell you that you can't achieve your goals. Let others envy become your

motivation. Live a fulfilled life, love everyone, lead

by positive examples, lend a helping hand and learn

from life lessons. When unwanted circumstances

surfaces and everyone appears befuddled, wicked

thoughts and negative actions promotes temptation

to deliver evil upon others. Every day that we are

alive and breathing, we should use each moment to

make everlasting memories to pass along to our

children, our children's' children and to anyone that

could benefit from our personal trials and

tribulations. I present to you my testimony in script

because I would like to be a reference point

throughout your lives. I want to help rebuild

confidence, boost your self-esteem, motivate your

dreams, reveal your self-worth and most

importantly restore your faith. In the game called life, select your teammates wisely. Strength may come in numbers, but power comes from prayers. Let's play a game of challenges/obstacles/detours: **You vs God**! How about football? Many females may not understand the game and even the die-hard female fans miss the focus of the game. I'm a Redskins fan who team are you cheering for? The clock is set:

Game clock: In God's eyes, the greatest heroes of faith are not those who achieve prosperity, success and power in this life; but those who treat life as a temporary assignment and serve faithfully, expecting their promise reward in eternity. The clock is ticking…your identity is in eternity and your homeland is in Heaven. You will not be in heaven seconds before you cry out, "Why did I put so much emphasis on things that was so temporary?"

Football: God will carry you through whatever you are going only if you trust Him, believe in Him, have faith I Him and love Him unconditionally. God is not just the starting point of your life, but the source of it. God wants you to sense his presence, but he's more concerned that you trust him than you feel him. Faith, not feelings, pleases God. If you want your life to have an impact than focus it.

Coach: Children, At Risk Youth, Young Adults, and Families, one who instructs the players in the fundamentals and directs the team strategies. God's purpose for his churches is identical to his purposes for you. Worship helps you focus on God; fellowship helps you face life's problems; discipleship helps you fortify your faith; ministry helps find your talents, and evangelism helps fulfill your mission. Attitude reflects leadership, so as a head coach you are highly valued as a man or woman of God. As the bible says, "As a face reflects in water so the heart will reflect the person".

Referee: Pastors, Parents, Educators, Professionals, Law Enforcement officials, you are all over the playing field in assuring that everyone is playing their position therefore; when a problem occurs make sure that during the review you allow God to be the final judge. Some of the equipment needed are but not limited to is a Bible, faith, strength, courage, integrity, and forgiveness.

The **mouth-piece** let the words and the meditation of one's heart be acceptable in thine sight. The **helmet** clearly puts God as the head of your life if you let him be in control. Your **uniform** is your protection. God is willing to be your knight and shining armor only if you fully believe and receive him as your Lord and Savior Jesus Christ. Shoes (**cleats**) are made to support you and to give you balance on the playing field however; ye I walk through the valley of the shadow of death, I will fear no evil.

Team: There are many teams in the league of football and people have their own preference as to who they like. But when that team isn't performing well to their liking than they are ready to disown the team and find another one that's winning. We would rather talk about winning, succeeding, overcoming and conquering than yielding, submitting, obeying and surrendering. So, if winning is everything than surrendering is unthinkable, but surrendering to God is the heart of worship.

In life, we will all face triumphs and that desire to have complete control. Real talk, this is the cause of so much stress in our lives because that struggle we have is really a struggle with God and there's no way we are going to win. So instead of trying harder, we need to trust more. I asked you again,

Authorized Personnel Only

who team are you on? In this game, **You v Him**

they are played by quarters, they consist of married

couples with children, divorced couples, single

parents and single individuals. Every quarter must

come to an end therefore; we are obligated to do our

very best in providing the bare necessities for our

household to function properly. It doesn't matter

what quarter you are in, no one else will ever be

able to play the role God has plan for you. So, if

you don't make the unique contribution to the body

of Christ than it won't be made. He has given is

begotten son to die on the cross for all our sins, so

believe that he is the only authorized personnel you

need to stay in contact to gain an all access pass.

The game of life already has started and it first

down.

The more God gives you the more responsible he expects you to become. Second down, it took Noah 120 years to build the ark so keep moving forward daily to give God your all. Now it's **halftime**, take this time to assess your life strategies/game plan to assist you with building your "FAITH" with God to finish in obedience. Listen to your coaches speak. There is no growth without change, no change without fear of loss and no loss without pain. The battle for sin is won or lost in your mind. Whatever gets your attention will get you! **Third down**, do whatever God ask of you without reservation or hesitation. Don't just say "I'll pray about it".

Fourth and final down God doesn't owe you an explanation or reason for everything he asks you to do. You are at a place now where you still haven't made it into the **end zone**, but you are close. **Field goal** attempt, God promise three rewards in eternity.

First, you will be given God's <u>affirmation</u>: He will say "Good job! Well done!" Next you will receive a <u>promotion</u> and be given greater responsibility in eternity. "I will put you in charge of many things." Then you will be <u>honored</u> with a celebration: Come and share your master's happiness." Yes, this is real. If you are still a little guarded than push the other team inside their end zone for a **safety**. I say to you surrender yourself to the Lord and wait patiently for him. He is good and loving. He is all powerful. He notices every detail of our lives. He is in control. He has a plan for our lives. And he is the only one who can save you! Still finding it difficult to grasp? **Penalties** than becomes a part of the game. See all sins at its root, is failing to give God glory. Love anything more than God. Refusing to bring glory to God is prideful, rebellion and it is the sin that caused Satan's fall and ours too. One question: Will you allow God to cover you starting today?

We all have had some setbacks in our daily lives that are often like **fumbles**. It is painful, but it is vital for the development of our faith. God knows we are incapable of being perfect or sinless. Each one of us was designed uniquely by God with talents, gifts, skills, and other abilities. God didn't give you your abilities for selfish purpose, they were given to benefit others. God uses everything for greater in our lives. Sometimes we must take a

time out. It is a test of our faith. Will you

continue to love, trust, obey and worship God, even

when you have no sense of his presence or visible

evidence of his work in our lives?

Touchdown...God is the Creator and Maker, Lord

and Master, Judge, Redeemer, Father, and Savior;

but most shocking truth is that-Almighty God

yearns to be your friend. Right now, God is inviting

each one of you to live for his glory, by fulfilling

the purpose he made you for. It's really the only

way to live. Everything else just exists. Real life

begins by committing yourself completely to Jesus

Christ. If you are not sure you have done this, all

you need to do is receive and believe. God's goal

for your life on earth is not comfort, but for character development. Your faith makes your righteous, by having faith for what Jesus has done for you. So, what do you have that God hasn't given you? And if you have it all from God, why boast as though you have accomplished anything on your own. **Game Over**!

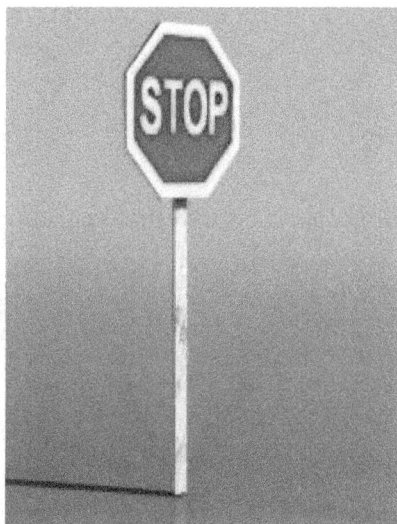

Stopping doesn't mean that you can't start again!

STOP

Working for someone else was something I had to do before working for myself. I wanted to enhance my nursing assistant skills and gain all the knowledge that I could about caring for sick individuals, especially children and the elderly. I became very good at my job and I always gave 110% to my patients and their love ones. I remember a special patient that I cared for truly touched my heart. It didn't matter how many patients I have on any given day; I was devoted to spending a little time with each one. This special patient was a child who had a very manageable illness. I must admit, I had him spoiled, he would cry for me and gave the rest of the staff a hard time to perform any type of procedure on him especially if he knew that I was working. On this evening, it

STOP

was time for my twelve-hour shift to end.
Something inside of me said go back into his room
and stay until he falls asleep. I used to tell him to be
good, not to cry, I would be back, and I would bring
him a popsicle. Everyone else used my lines to try
and gain his trust, but it wasn't that easy for them to
do. That night, I sat in his room and held him in my
arms and sang "There's a God who knows is all".
Now, I'm not a singer, but I believe I did alright,
either he went to sleep to tune out my trembling
voice or the words from my mouth soothe his little
body and hopefully eased his pain. Finally, he was
asleep. I laid him in his crib-like bed, secured the
rails and began to walk towards the door. As I
reached the door, I looked back and blew him a soft
kiss and waved whispering night, night. The staff

STOP

thought I had already left because it was well passed my quitting time. I turned and looked at the nurse and said do you really think that he would be this quiet, knowing I'm still here. We laughed it off as I clocked out. The next morning, I arrived to work and while walking down the hallway, I immediately noticed a large pool of doctors, nurses, the social worker, the Director of Nursing, other staff member and the police gathered around the nurses' station. They were standing there in almost a complete silence. I approached the staff room door, it swung open and it was the nurse that I laughed with the night before. She pulled me into the staff room and said I got something to tell you. She looked as if she saw a ghost. Her face was as white as the pair of scrubs she was wearing. I knew

STOP

it was something serious. What? What? What's
going on out there? She stated, your little buddy is
gone. Gone? What do you mean, he's gone? She
shrugged my shoulders, like I shrugged my
mother's shoulders when the doctor delivered us
such bad news. She yelled out, Denise he's dead. I
didn't believe her, and I tried to break free to go to
his room. She slapped me hard enough to bring my
attention back into focus. I mentally broke down
and it was at that moment it happened…my heart
felt like it stopped again. My heart cried more than
my eyes. Screams were whaling on the inside of me
searching for a way out, it felt like it was bursting
through my stomach causing my small and large
intestines to suffocate. I needed oxygen! My mind
was echoing breathe, breathe, breathe…finally, I

released what felt like my last breath. I became the

walking dead at that moment. I knew that after

losing my little buddy, working there would be very

difficult for me to handle. Some say that you

shouldn't get close to your patients, but how can

you not, if the passion and compassion comes from

within you. Losing people that we know, and love

happens all the time, but when the unexpected death

of a child it's never going to be easy to cope with. I

needed a way out. It seemed as everything I loved

was slowly being taken away from me, even the

ones that I barely knew. I began considering starting

my own business, working with residents in the

comfort of their homes. I believe that old saying,

"once an adult and twice a child". I knew that it

didn't matter what I did, I could never replace my

STOP

little buddy. So, I chose to work with the big babies-

the elderly. I launched my business

B.L.E.S.S.I.N.G.S which stood for **b**eautiful **li**ves

enduring **s**erious **s**uffering **i**s **n**ow **g**aining **s**upport!

Plan, prepare and produce. I had an updated resume

prepared, my business cards, flyers, and email

account and most importantly legal authorization

from the Secretary of State of South Carolina office

acknowledging that my business was successfully

incorporated. I started searching the local

newspaper for potential clients and one ad stood out

to me. I started to delay calling the number provided

because I was out on a mini vacation still clearing

my head before I got back into my work mode. I

decided to make the call and spoke with one the

client's legal guardians. The telephone call went

very well. We spoke about our military careers, our

children, our families, my credentials and my

passion for wanting to help individuals that's

disabled and vulnerable that needs TLC.

The call lasted for approximately ten minutes she

was very impressed with my tone and kindhearted

personality as well as my resume. I was excited to

meet the guardian(s) and the potential client. The

day of my interviewed, I felt great! I said to myself

that this feels right, so I'm claiming it. I arrived

approximately fifteen minutes early and I was

greeted with smiles, hugs and kisses in the

driveway. So far so good. I entered the home looked

over at "granny" sitting in a recliner chair with her

head hung down and her body language screaming

STOP

please move me over to the other side. The
caretaker was trying to feed her some lunch, but she
wasn't eating. Immediately, I sprang into action. I
asked the caretaker if I may assist by taking her
place she kindly agreed. She said good luck because
she doesn't eat well anymore. In my mind, I knew
this was my moment of truth to show my skills and
offer my tender touch to such a frail little body. I
introduced myself to granny and the sound of a
different voice, she tried to hold her head up, and so
I stooped down on one knee so that she could see
my face. Granny reached out and touched my hand.
I asked her for permission to readjust her position
and to continue with her meal before it got cold.
She gave me a smile and said thank you sweetie. I
could hear the grand daughter in the background

STOP

sniffling and talking on her cell phone. The receiver
on the other end of the call heard nothing but great
things about me and I hadn't had the sit-down
interview yet. Granny finished her meal even
though I had to serve it to her in smaller portion
because her swallowing mechanism wasn't as
functional as it used to be. I padded her recliner
with more pillows to relieve direct pressure on her
derriere and to make her feel comfortable. The
granddaughter asked, when would I like to start. I
apologize for delaying my interview and that's
when it happened…. she took my hand and said.
Denise, after what my granny did for you and you
just got here; we don't need to see anything further.
How soon would you like to start working? Let's
talk about your pay and bonus. Honestly, I knew I

would have aced my interview, but the additional hands-on was just what I did best. I stayed there approximately two hours, I was given more information regarding her medical condition and all her directives in case of an emergency. I accepted the position with ease. The guardian shared with me that she had already interview sixteen other people and some were license therapists, retired nurses and one individual had a master's degree in psychology. All I had was my nursing assistant certification, six years' experience, a revolving mind, an open heart and my integrity. I didn't entertain the work days or the rate of pay, but I did have one question. Why me? The guardian quickly responded by saying because God sent you to our granny and now she's your granny too! That was good enough for me. She

STOP

only confirmed what God had already said what is

for you, is for you. And because I had been praying

about this day to come I wasn't going to worry

about it. Trust God wholeheartedly he will not fail

you. God was so good to me my net pay was near

$1500.00 bi-weekly. I'm grateful for all that God

has allowed me to do. The things that "granny" had

stopped doing, over a short time period she was

doing those things and more. Because of her health,

she had not been out of the house therefore she

received all her care at home. Well for Mother's

Day that year, I invited my daughter out with me

and Granny for dinner and ice cream. The

granddaughters were overwhelmed with joy and I

think I sensed a little bit of jealously too. I became a

part of the family! I worked with Granny for nearly

STOP

two years before a relative moved in with her
convincing two of the three guardians that she could
give her better care and that they didn't need to pay
that much money for her personal care to someone
else.

This became a huge battle between three legal
guardians. Let's just say when money is involved
everyone may not have the same agenda in mind.
My journey had come to an end working with
Granny, but our love was unchangeable! It had only
been a couple of months that had passed since my
departure; she slipped away in her sleep. I was
notified by one of the guardians via telephone. The
news was devastating. I had a flashback to my little
buddy. I looked towards the sky and thanked God

STOP

for giving me the opportunity again to make a

positive change in her life even if the timing was

limited. I do believe that it was meant for me to

work one on one with her to take her back to that

happy place where she once was before her health

started to fail. God put this union together; he had

made a perfect match, Granny who was a

millionaire and myself who's mind and heart that's

worth far more than that…. is rich in love! Listen,

it doesn't matter who you are, where you are, and or

what you are doing. When God is in control of your

spirit & soul your body will obey him and his

words. Never doubt him because he is God

Almighty and he's worthy. Never allow someone

else to tell you it's' not going to work because

either they tried it or someone they know tried it

STOP

and it didn't work for them. Understand that God knows it all. You have not, if you ask not. Trust him because he is greater in you, than you alone. Blessing have been showering down from Heaven ever since. I acknowledged him and accepted him as the head of my life. Our God is the way, the truth and the light! When darkness comes don't be afraid for he is with you. If you don't have everything that you want, don't worry because he supplies your every need. Step out on faith, build a solid foundation with our Heavenly Father and stand firm on his word and wait on your blessings. Patience is of a virtue!

JUNCTION

When two or more people touch and agree God is in

the mist!

Junction

Job Corps was a very rewarding place to work because each day I had the opportunity to make a positive difference in young adults lives that had no clear vision as to which way to turn. A normal day wasn't an eight to five job. I would work until I have completed my assignments for that day. Often, I would get so caught up in my work until I've lost track of time and everyone else was gone for the day except me. Students would often stop by my office just to say hello, thank you or needing sound advice. However; I managed to get plenty of work done. On Wednesdays, I held orientation sessions whereas; I would present the Job Corp overall programs utilizing the benefits as a sells pitch to attract prospective applicants. One of the challenges that I looked forward to excelling in recruitment to receive occasional bonuses. I can recall this one

applicant very vividly because he made sure I didn't

forget his name and his reason(s) for wanting to be

a part of the center's life. I must admit that I was

intrigued therefore; my goal was to process his

information as quickly and as thoroughly as

possible. Each day my work was cut out for me and

to top it all off on the busiest day of the week, I was

given a short notice that my office had to move to

another building. We did not have movers, so it was

a do-it-yourself project. I dread the thought but

embrace the fact that I would have my own private

space. So, my colleague and I formulated a plan by

readjusting our daily planners to move both offices

at the same time. We made a tedious process fun,

exciting, and if I must say we receive a free

workout wearing heels. We spent days of stacking

and lifting heavy boxes, pushing and pulling dollies,

carrying office equipment and furniture, cleaning

and shredding documents finally, I was moved. I

almost put in a request for a transfer to work in the

materials & distributions department because I felt I

had mastered those skills. There was no time to

complain because I had to get back on track starting

with returning what appeared to be at least 100

telephone calls. Days had turned into weeks passed

and I get an unexpected visitor. Yes, it was that

young man who was so adamant about jump

starting his career. He came by to check on the

status of his application. I could not give him an

update because my new office was still half packed

and disorganized. I can still remember that look of

Junction

disappointment on his face and I felt as if I let him
down. I informed him that I had already started the
process, but I was taken off course due to the
sudden move. My words are equivalent to a savings
bond. So, I made a promise to him to give me two
weeks and I would have a start date for him. He
replied, "I guess I'll go and tell my dad what's
happening". So, I asked was his father on the center
with him and he said, yes ma'am, he's sitting in the
car. I asked him to get his father and I would
explain what occurred and take responsibility for
the delay with his application. He smiled and left
my new office. Moments later an unidentified male
appeared in the door frame. At first, I was looking
downward reviewing paperwork, but his presence
blocked the lighting that entered my office from the

Junction

hallway, so I looked up and my eyes immediately
connected with his and both of us appeared startled
for just a brief second as if we welcomed this outer
body, out of mind experience. He kindly extended
his right hand and introduced himself as Mr. Darryl
Williams Sr. and although he already knew my
name, I stated my name and title as I gripped his
hand squeezing it as if, I was holding on for dear
life. I know what you all maybe thinking and yes, I
do agree, something got a hold of me. However, I
was very polite and kept it very professional. I knew
the information that I had wanted to share with him
regarding his son's application, but it appears I
could not open my mouth to let the words out. The
Jaws of Life would not have been successful on its
first attempt. Mr. Williams, I said please let me

explain. He interceded and stated that it was okay because after seeing my shuffled office he could understand the delay. Well, I thought to myself, oh my, this isn't going to be easy. Somehow, I still felt guilty because I was that Admission's Counselor that always tried to be at the top of my game. And my words were like a savings bond. I decided to walk him back to the parking lot and continued the conversation. I could not live with myself if I did not act on behalf of our unique encounter. Let's just say that I used another tactically tool to secretly interrogate him. I never had this happened to me before in my life so yes, it was worth a shot. I continued laying out my personal line of questions when he kindly threw a few back at me. I knew I had an intelligent man walking alongside of me, so

Junction

he decided to cut to the chase and asked his son DJ
to tell me his marital status. DJ replied, no ma'am
my dad has been divorced now for over six years.
Well, I guess this isn't going to be as difficult as I
thought. So, we exchanged phone numbers and I
stood aside and watched them drive off. I went
directly to my colleague's office shut her office
door and sat down looking as if I was I just found
out that I won the Mega Million lottery. I remember
hearing her say, oh my God, girl you are glowing.
What's going on? I replied: I think I'm in love.
Believe me I couldn't believe what I was saying
myself. This was not a typical day on the job. I
returned to my office locked my door and sat down
in my chair shaking like a leaf on a tree, looking
towards the ceiling asking God to reveal to me the

meaning behind my mysterious behavior. I waited
and waited no answer from him. I began thinking
back over the events that took place from the
moment he stepped in my doorway. Than it
happened....

God reminded me that I was single, and I always
prayed and said that I would wait on him to send me
my King. I knew that I was a strong minded, well-
educated, beautiful woman regardless of the battles
that I've had. I won some and some were lost, but
through it all God never left my side. On March 3,
2011, my life changed ever. Mr. Williams invited
me to an all seafood fest that he was having. All I
knew about Beaufort, South Carolina was that I
drove there once a month to conduct monthly

Junction

presentations for Job Corp. I'm a seafood lover so I
gladly accepted his invitation. Here it was
Wednesday, and I had merely a day and a half to
digest all of this and or time to call it off. I knew
that I needed to get one more opinion, so that
evening I called my one and only
cousin/sister/girlfriend Tee. She listened to my story
and after careful deliberation; she brought me right
back to the source of it.... God. I sat quietly and
finally realized that this bizarre encounter was no
mistake. I looked towards the sky and said Lord, I
thank you for all that you have done, is doing and
will do in my professional and personal life. It
seemed as if Friday came before Thursday. Mr.
Williams and I stayed in touch since the day we
met. I prayed prior to leaving my home. I then

Junction

asked God again if this trip was not in my best interested to please give me a sign.

I forgot to mention that a week earlier I had to take my Infiniti G20 to get a diagnostic test because it started shutting off and the check engine light stayed on. They reset the light and said that the problem could have started because my fuel cap wasn't tightened. Two days later, I spent nearly one hundred and fifty dollars because the light was back on and the car shut off again. So, I was nervous thinking that my vehicle would probably stop on me before I reached my destination or that I make it there and realize that I'm uncomfortable and I need to get the hell out of there and my car won't start. My car is my lifeline in this case. Anyway, I

Junction

procrastinated until around 6:30pm and finally I said what's for me, is for me and my heavenly father would not mislead me nor forsake me. I got into my car a drove off. My cousin had all of Darryl's pertinent information such as his full name, date of birth, make and model of his truck, physical street address, post office box address, and a good physical description of him. Also, if needed my colleague and or manager could access my files to retrieve his social security number if things really took a wrong turn. You may think that this is over reacting but look at the current statistics of crimes against females specifically by someone they know, or should I say think they know. The engine light never came on nor did my car shut off, the drive there was as smooth as riding solo in a limousine. I

Junction

notified my cousin that I arrived safely, and she told
me to enjoy myself and to know that she was on
standby. I was greeted by his son and his brother Al.

A warm feeling overwhelmed my body as if God
was assuring me that I was covered by his blood.
Darryl greeted me with a hug and a soft kiss to my
forehead. Oh, how sweet, I was properly introduced
to the family members and one of his best friends,
Eric. His youngest son had asked me to promise
him something; but I told him that I needed to know
what he wanted me to promise before I could make
such a commitment. He said would you promise to
be my mommy and never leave me, I was lost for
words, my heart sunk to the middle of my stomach
and the emotional feeling brought tears to my eyes.

Junction

I paused, I didn't want to hurt him so I immediately as God to give me the right words to say. Finally, I responded baby, I promise regardless to what happens between your dad and me, I will always want to be a part of your life. He gave me a hug and a kiss on my cheek and said thank you. Priceless! If this wasn't enough to change the mood try adding to the fact that I was about to meet his mother. OMG! I didn't know what to think, so I asked him was he sure that he wanted to do that. He said yes because his son had already told her the story of how we met and how beautiful I was and that I was coming to visit. After hearing all that I felt a little uncomfortable because I was not dressed to meet his mom. I was dressed to eat seafood. Together we walked the short distance to her house holding

Junction

hands like two teenagers already in love. He held

the door as I entered, and she greeted me with open

arms. I will never forget her words: welcome baby,

I have heard so much about you. I have an extra

room here if you would like to stay here so that you

don't have to take that long drive back tonight; also,

remember in this family once you're in, you're in

and when you're out your out!

The night was everything that said, "family time". I

was having so much fun, I forgot to check back in

with my cousin. She had called and text my phone

and left me a couple of voice messages voicing her

concern. When I called her back, she was relieved

to hear my voice and happy that I was enjoying

myself. Seafood, music, games and laughter all

Junction

together in a friendly atmosphere at the same time.
The night was going by so fast, I regretted leaving
my house so late. His brother and sister both offered
me to be their house guest that night. I felt like I
belonged. Darryl captured my thoughts without me
even saying a word. That spark was still in our eyes.
We had so much fun I ended up staying the entire
weekend and he brought me a new outfit for work
that Monday. I must say that he treated me just like
the queen God said I was and I was ready to crown
him as my king. Time continues to pass and every
day we lived just to talk to each other. We had so
much in common. We were both single parents and
very protective of our children, we both served in
the military, and we both have a love for football.
Although I'm a Washington Redskins fan and he's a

Junction

New York Jets fan, we support each other's team if we're not playing against one another. I went back to work feeling blessed and full of energy. The seafood was on point!! During the day while at work, we would be thinking about each other than be would be dialing the numbers at the same time. There's something in this for the both of us. Our paths have crossed for a reason. God has brought us across cities and counties through communication. I have found a lifetime friend. Darryl and I continued to build a stronger relationship daily. We became so close if I had a rough day at work or was feeling ill he could tell by the tone of my voice what was wrong. I didn't know if his United States Naval training had anything to do with his exceptional ability to detect unhappiness. Three months later after a short conversation we decided to take our

relationship to another level. Again, I stepped out

on faith and left Orangeburg, South Carolina and

moved to Beaufort. His son was doing well at Job

Corp. I can't believe that a year has passed. We

were still very happy and in deeply love. Darryl

proposed to me one evening while one of my

favorite nephew's (CJ) was visiting us from Florida.

I knew that he was a God-fearing man that was

made especially for me, so the proposal was

expected, but I just didn't know exactly when it was

going to happen. Of course, I said yes! We went on

a cruise to the Bahamas along with his family for

their routine family reunion trip. It was my first

time visiting the Bahamas and Darryl made certain

that it would be the one I will never forget. I

stepped out on faith and God covered me every step

of the way. We as women long to have someone

who will treat us how a woman should be treated

but the problem lies in the fact that we often must

go through two or more different relationships to

get a little of all these qualities a man should have.

Some males prefer to use forms of abuse to get a

woman to knowledge him and or obey him. And

women that have seen such misguided trust and

authority at an early age feel that this is the way a

man should act. Gentlemen & Ladies if you have

ever experience abuse on any level understand that

it is "never" ok! You owe it to yourselves to be

accepted for who you and what you are yet to

become. If you have children make sure you put

their health and safety first! Love yourself enough

Junction

to know that God has already shown just how much he loves everybody. He gave his only begotten son, who died on the cross for our sins. Use caution when you approach a man that wants to be is control over your life. There is no "u" turn in a one-way relationship. Stop and think what would Jesus do? The road of life can take you in a circular intersection then suddenly you've reached a junction. If you're not sure which way to go yield and take the road using the authorized personnel only. This is God almighty asking you to allow him to be the driver as you proceed on your journey. Put all your problems in God's hands or as some older ones would say leave them on the tracks. If you follow his map you will not run into a dead end. His way is the highway to Heaven.

Junction

But when you trust God and believe that he will

provide your every need that special someone will

appear when you least expect it. A good man his not

the one who dress like a model, talks like an actor,

or sings like an artist. He is one that appreciates the

things God has granted him to have through hard

work and by spending time to get to know himself

better. A God fear man will say not what's on his

mind but what's in his heart. I used to laugh at

females when they would say that they fell in love

at first sight. I can honestly say that I am a firm

believer that falling in love at first sight can happen.

Thinking back to the day we met in my office and

our eyes connected, we could view a screenshot of

our names written on each other's hearts. The last

names became visible when I changed my name to

Junction

Williams. Wedding bells rang on October 20, 2013,
I married my best friend. Our wedding was held on
the same weekend as his family reunion. My unique
theme shared all the things that were created in the
beginning of what we have built together. Our
theme: "A Moment to Treasure". The décor
consisted of chocolate, ivory & turquoise silk
colored linen and rose petals, treasure chests filled
with jewels, crystal clear Eiffel tower vases holding
a single yellow mum flower and a picture frame
displaying one of these single words: love, peace,
happiness, faith, trust, hope, blessings, forgiveness,
patience, family, friends, joy, compassion, courage,
and strength. Our vows were not written nor
rehearsed. They came straight from the heart. Our
children gave us away to each other. My oldest son

Junction

had a tire blowout on the interstate trying to get to the wedding on time. I was only told that he had an accident and that he was fine, but he would be late. I cried all the way down the aisle because he was not by my side. He made it safely, but after the photo session was initially over the photographer stay so that he could capture some images of us with my son and his family. We celebrated our fourth wedding anniversary on October 20, 2017 and our love is still fresh as the day our eyes allowed us to see in each other's hearts. Artist, Cleo Higgins said it best in her song, "Love was Made for Us". We can talk about anything and pray about everything together. God is the head of our lives and we are joined together at the heart!

Junction

Darryl   Denise

A Moment to Treasure"

October 20, 2013

We **never would have made it** if it had not been for

our Lord and Savior Jesus Christ. Today is our

wedding day so **let's get married**. *No weapon*

formed against us shall prosper. Darryl/Denise, *I*

promise that *I will always love you* because your

actions have spoken louder than your words. Darryl,

there is **something in my heart** that makes me

believe you when you said that I am *forever your*

lady and *I don't wanna share* your love with

anyone else. We both agreed that the time is now so

let's **go get it**. *For you I will*, our love is true

because God has brought us through many trials and

tribulations from across countries, land, seas, states, counties and cities. I know *I gotta be* the one just for you.

Over time *I've learned to respect the power of love.* Now I would also like to say *thank you* for loving my children and family as your very own. Today, I vowed to *give all my love to you* because *you complete me* and *I love you more every day*, therefore; *for the love that I gave, I pray* no matter what storm comes in our pathway, we will continue to stand by God's holy word in faith, hope and love until the sun rises again saying *I'm going be ready*!!!!

Travel with God and you will never go in the wrong

direction!

TruKolors' Prayer

Dear Heavenly Father, we come before you not on bending knees, but with our heads bows and our hearts wide open. We thank you for allowing your Angels to watch over us last night and to bring us to see this day. We give you all the Glory and the Praise because without you we are nothing. Lord, open the flood gates to heaven and let it rain on us. Give us the knowledge to make better decisions that will impact our daily lives as we continue to grow spiritually and in *Prosperity*. We come before you today oh Lord, not to ask for riches nor fame, but for us to allow the Royalty of your love be at the center of our hearts. Because you are the way, we want to follow you. You are the truth, so tell us what we need to know and because you are the light, let your TruKolors' shine so bright that every mankind will be able to see that you are using our good for your greater. Through Christ Jesus all things are possible; but good works without Faith is dead. Lord, we ask that you cover us with thy blood and allow no weapons formed against us to prosper. In Jesus name, we pray Amen!

One-Way

TruKolors', Incorporation was uniquely designed to support families who have endured the loss of a child and or for children who's battling a terminal illness in South Carolina. Our nonprofit organization offers TruKolors care packages designed as an impactful keepsake to bring them a level of comfort during these life changing experiences.

This organization was solely created in loving memory of my niece who had a brain tumor. One hour and eighteen minutes just shy of her eighteenth birthday, she entered eternal rest. We will never know her full potential; but what I do know is that her academic achievements were superior. Her spirituality presented itself at an early age. Her

One-Way

smile gives me the strength and courage to step out on faith to keep her memory alive. I am ready, willing and able to take a stand to allow her radiant smile shine down from heaven through a ray of colors.

I believe that if she could speak to me from heaven, she would say, "I give myself away, so you can use me". Lady Justice has often been depicted wearing a blindfold like the one that was pulled over the law eyes back then. The blindfold represents objectivity in that Justice is or should be meted out objectivity, without fear or favor, regardless of identity, money, power, or weakness; blind justice and impartially.

Color should be defined equally as this tradition in our society because without color we would all

One-Way

blind! Dr. Martin Luther King said it best. "Let us all hope that the dark clouds of racial prejudice will soon pass away, and that in some not too distant tomorrow the radiant stars of love and brotherhood will shine over our great nation with all their scintillating beauty." Our nation has suffered many horrific tragedies current to this day". I'm only one in a million that wants to bring about positive change remember guns don't just kill people; people with guns kill people. TruKolors' was incorporated on August 13, 2012, four months and a day on December 14, 2012, my heart was deeply saddened. In Newton, Connecticut, a lone gunman entered the Sandy Hook Elementary school shot and killed six adults and twenty children. I know there's nothing I can do that would bring back these innocent lives; but I can help keep their memories alive because this is what my niece would have wanted. Several of TruKolors' associates participated in the MLK Day parade that was held in Beaufort, South Carolina on January 16, 2013. And in honor of Dr. King's vision of unity, instead of us carrying our TruKolors' banner, we designed a banner with twenty-six candles displaying all of the victims' names from Sandy Hook Elementary. Our organization have seven colors that represents the vision statement of TruKolors', Inc. These colors display a spiritual connection to me.

1. **Blue**-Heavenly-In my Father's house is many mansions; if it were not so I would

2. have told you. I go to prepare a place for you. *(John 14:2).*

3. **Green**-Prosperity-Give and it will be given to you. Good measure, pressed down, shaken together, running over, will be put into your lap. For with the measure you use it will be measured back to you. *(Luke 6:38).*

4. **Orange**-Praise-Saying with a loud voice, worthy is the Lamb that was slain to receive power and riches, and wisdom, and strength and glory, and blessings. *(Revelations: 5:12).*

5. **Pink**-Faith-Now faith is the substance of things hoped for, the evidence of things not seen. *(Hebrew 11:1).*

6. **Purple**-Royalty-Go through, go through the gates, prepare ye the way of the people; cast up, cast up the highway; gather out the stones; lift a standard for the people. *(Isaiah 62:10).*

7. **White**-Angels-Likewise, I say unto you, there is joy in the presence of the angels of God over one sinner that repents. *(Luke 15:10).*

8. **Yellow**-Glory-A man ought not to cover his head, since he is the image and glory of God; but the woman is the glory of man. *(1 Corinthians 11:7)*

One-Way

The roads that I've traveled on showed me all these colorful signs that you see every day, and not once did I recognize their connection. Traveling from one location to the next known or unknown destination start observing the clues, because the traffic signs are like flash points of life mysteries that only you can discover. I never would have made it through if it had not been for my faith and forgiveness and I continuously give thanks to my Lord and Savior because he keeps on blessing me.

Traveling Ties that Bind

To God be the Glory. My book of poems **"VOICELESS"** are spoken words to help comfort bereaved families. Just imagined if Heaven could allow you to hear the voices of your loved ones. These poems offer a personalize message for their families. Everyone should be on a highway to heaven as they travel on this journey called "life". There are many lifesaving and warning signs posted along the way. However, it's up to you to recognize them, read them, relate to them and make the right choices.

Writing poetry is only one of my many talents that God has blessed me with. I will continue to write until that that day comes when someone else will be writing for me. Remember, our lives here on earth is only temporary!

Sundays

Hello, my brother, I just called to ask how was your day

I'm still on the road, but I will see y'all on Sunday

All the days of my life there's none better than this one

God chose me to join him to ride the clouds over the
moon and just pass the sun

Monday's was just the typical day to start my week

I drove hours and hours during the daylight leaving me
little to no time to sleep

Tuesday's, I tried to get organized by planning a better
routine

Wednesday's came so quickly, I forgot half of the things
I said and most of what I had seen

Somehow, I made it over and by Thursday my body is so
tired, I just want to close my eyes

I can't because there's one more day to go before I can
say goodbye

Friday, my work week is done and I'm looking forward
to making my way back home

Its Saturday, my day off finally I'm resting comfortably,
it didn't matter if I was home alone

Sunday is my favorite day because I get to praise God
and be with the ones that I love

Every day from now on will be like Sunday because now
I'm working fulltime for our Savior above

"SIP, Uncle Jun"

Pay close attention to all signs!

******

The images displayed in this book are not clear as one would expect to see. Because if God allowed us to see his power in advance, how strong would your faith be? Drive safely!

www.ingramcontent.com/pod-product-compliance
Lightning Source LLC
LaVergne TN
LVHW051041080426
835508LV00019B/1640